NONA BAUER

New Hampshire Backroads

by William G. Scheller

American Geographic Publishing

Helena, Montana

DAVID A. WHITE

ISBN 0-938314-56-4
© 1989 American Geographic Publishing, P.O. Box 5630, Helena, MT 59604. (406) 443-2842.
William A. Cordingley, Chairman
Rick Graetz, Publisher & CEO
Mark Thompson, Director of Publications
Barbara Fifer, Production Manager

American Geographic Publishing is a corporation for publishing illustrated geographic information and guides. It is not associated with American Geographical Society. It has no commercial or legal relationship to and should not be confused with any other company, society or group using the words geographic or geographical in its name or its publications.

Text © 1989 William G. Scheller.
Design by Linda Collins.
Printed in Hong Kong by Dai Nippon Printing Co., San Francisco.

NONA BAUER

ABOUT THE AUTHOR

William G. Scheller is the author of 11 books and more than 100 magazine articles, including American Geographic Publishing's *New Hampshire: Portrait of the Land and Its People* (1988). Since 1970, he has made his home in Vermont and Massachusetts, and has traveled and vacationed extensively in New Hampshire. Mr. Scheller is a former editor of *Appalachia,* the journal of the Appalachian Mountain Club, an organization that maintains its field headquarters and a chain of back-country huts in the White Mountains.

Contents

Facing page: Fishing the Connecticut River near Pittsburg.

Title page: The tugboat fleet at Portsmouth.
Page 2, left: Mt. Washington Hotel at Bretton Woods.
Right: Near Hollis.
Page 3, left: Lake Umbagog.
Right: In Bretton Woods.

Front cover: Walpole on the Connecticut River. NONA BAUER
Back cover, left: Covered bridge at Jackson. NORMAN E. EGGERT
Right: Whitefield. DAVID A. WHITE

1 Portsmouth
The Soul of a Seafaring Town

There sits the *Albacore*, high and dry, with a dent in its nose and a permanent gangplank fixed to the side. This was the first blimp-shaped submarine, the first built along the modern lines that succeeded those of the flat-decked submersibles of two world wars, and its counter-rotating propellors drove it through the water at a record speed still classified by the Navy. Launched in 1953, the U.S.S. *Albacore* spent 19 years in commissioned service not only without firing a shot in anger, but also without the wherewithal to fire any shots at all. Built and sent to sea purely for experimental purposes, *Albacore* earned its keep by proving the seaworthiness and maneuverability of the tuna-like teardrop hull.

In 1985 the decommissioned *Albacore* was brought back to Portsmouth, the city where it was launched. The sub's last voyage took it past the Portsmouth Navy Yard and up the Piscataqua to a man-made channel—closed and filled after the job was done—that led to a dry berth in Albacore Park, off Market Street a few blocks west of downtown. Here visitors can board the sub and take a guided tour through living quarters and work stations (efficiently compact or insufferably claustrophobic, depending on one's point of view) once shared by 55 men.

The *Albacore* is an altogether appropriate place to begin a tour of Portsmouth itself—and not merely because it is the first attraction encountered along the road from Interstate 95, the usual route travelers take to the city and the centuries-old precincts along the waterfront. Anyone who wishes to know Portsmouth should first come to terms with its nautical traditions, of which *Albacore* is only a recent manifestation. Portsmouth is a city brought to life by the sea, by the pursuit of maritime commerce and naval defense. Now well into its fourth century, it successively has struggled through obscurity, grown rich on international trade, settled into genteel dilapidation and been born again as a paradigm of gentrification and New England prosperity, late–20th-century style. But down through all of its years, it has been a seaport first and foremost.

It was at the future site of Portsmouth that an Englishman first dropped anchor in New Hampshire waters. The year was 1603, and the visitor was Captain Martin Pring, master of the vessels *Speedwell* and *Discoverer*. Pring didn't linger at the mouth of the Piscataqua, and neither did Samuel de Champlain, who stopped by in 1605 while exploring the coastline south of his Nova Scotia base of operations.

The first party of colonists to establish a settlement in the vicinity of Portsmouth was led by David Thompson, who arrived just south of the Piscataqua at Odiorne's Point in 1623. Within a year, there was a small community on the south shore of the river's ample and well protected harbor. These settlers, who had come to the New Hampshire coast under the auspices of Britain's royally-chartered Council for New England and its grantholders John Mason and Fernando Gorges, were joined in 1631 by a group of Massachusetts planters—precursors, one might say, of a modern-day trend in migration from the Bay State to the Granite State. The Massachusetts men secured a charter whereby they called their community Piscataqua, a name soon changed to Strawberry Bank (this appellation is preserved today, in its 17th-century spelling, at the restored town-within-a-town of Strawbery Banke). Finally, in 1653, Portsmouth became Portsmouth. In keeping with the political realities of the time, the town's incorporation and name change were ratified not by any New Hampshire authority but by the General Court of Massachusetts. In 1641, the fledgling communities between the Merrimack and the Piscataqua had cast their lot with the older and larger colony. This marriage of convenience would last nearly four decades.

But regardless of where it sent its elected representatives, Portsmouth's business—as Melville and the Old Testament might have put it—was upon great waters. Its earliest maritime occupation was fishing; in fact, for centuries before the arrival of the

---

Facing page: *An oil tanker departs Portsmouth harbor, assisted by a tug. The sailboat is farther from the tanker than the camera seems to indicate.*

Work and play in Portsmouth harbor: lobsterman and windsurfer near New Castle, east of the city.

English, Portuguese and Breton fishermen had dried and salted their catches of cod at temporary staging areas along this part of the New England coast. As both coastal and inland settlements multiplied in the 1600s, though, Portsmouth found itself more and more in demand as a conduit through which supplies from abroad passed to the interior, and native natural resources took ship for England. One of the earliest and most important "crops" shipped from Portsmouth was the seemingly endless supply of masts cut from the pine forests of the Piscataqua basin, consigned to the growing British Navy.

Soon enough Portsmouth was building ships of its own, first for its mercantile and fishing fleets, and later for coastal defense: at the close of the 17th century, the French possessions to the north still were to be feared. Commerce, though, always has been New England's special form of warfare, and the oceangoing tonnage that slid down Portsmouth's ways increasingly was destined to receive cargoes of lumber, molasses, rum, spices, sugar and textiles. The greatest era of seagoing enterprise for Portsmouth and its merchant shipowners was the period from the close of the American Revolution through the first half of the 19th century, from the unshackling of New England from British trading strictures to the decline of smaller ports in the face of competition from New York and its Erie Canal link to the American heartland. (The Jeffersonian embargo, in the years immediately prior to the War of 1812, also dampened New England's international trading activity and even stirred regional sympathy for secession from the Union.)

The halcyon years of Portsmouth's seagoing commerce, before the war of 1812, were the years when the city's great Federal-style mansions were built, and when the magnificoes who built them kept liveried servants and gave grand entertainments. Until 1808 Portsmouth was New Hampshire's political as well as economic capital, and the protocols and intrigues of the governor's office and legislature lent even more of an air of importance to the place. By the time Portsmouth began its long slide from promi-

nence, there was plenty of material evidence to show what it had been, plenty left to refurbish and show off when the renascence finally came.

One constant throughout the ups and downs of Portsmouth's economic history has been the Portsmouth Naval Shipyard. Now a maintenance and repair center for navy vessels (the last new ships were launched here in the 1960s), the shipyard once was key to America's naval defense preparedness—particularly in the realm of submarines. The first modern U.S. submersible, the L8, was built at the yard during the first World War; during the second global conflict, fully half of American submarines were products of the Portsmouth Naval Shipyard. (At one point, the yard's output averaged more than two dozen of the craft each year). And, of course, Portsmouth launched the *Albacore*—the only one of its subs to come home to stay.

If you continue heading toward downtown on Market Street, past the Chamber of Commerce Information Center and the new Sheraton Hotel (built of red brick, out of deference to the prevailing material of the central commercial district), you come to one of Portsmouth's best-preserved reminders of the days of ship-owning merchant princes. The Moffatt-Ladd House is an exquisite work of Georgian architecture, a stately old mansion built to command a view of the Piscataqua and the respect of yeomen and gentry alike during the years just prior to the Revolution. As only such houses can, it smells of old money.

When the old money that built the Moffatt-Ladd House was new, it wasn't much by today's standards. Twelve thousand dollars was what it cost Captain John Moffatt to have his builders raise these walls, during the years 1758-1763, and fill them with the finest woodcarving, plasterwork and wallpaper. But Moffatt, a former captain in the mast trade and by middle age a well-to-do shipowner, wasn't building for himself. The house was a wedding present for his son, Samuel, and his bride Catharine Mason.

The younger Moffatts moved into their new residence early in 1764, but their tenure was not to be a long one. Although his father had been able to give him not only a fine house but also a Harvard education (Class of 1758), Samuel Moffatt doesn't appear to have inherited the older man's business sense. Within five years of his marriage and establishment in his mansion, Samuel was so far behind with his creditors that a hasty departure from Portsmouth seemed the only alternative to debtors' prison. He fled to the West Indies, where he later was joined by his wife and sons, and left his father to salvage ownership of the house from the wreckage of his estate. John Moffatt must have been glad he built his son's wedding present as well as he did, because it became his own home for the remainder of his 94 years. He shared the house with his daughter, Catherine, and her husband William Whipple, another wealthy ship owner who signed the Declaration of Independence and attained the rank of major general in the Revolutionary War. The Whipples left no heirs, and when John Moffatt died his grandson—son of Samuel—sold the house to his own sister's husband, a Dr. Haven, whereupon it became a wedding present once again. The Havens gave it to their daughter, who married a man named Ladd, and their son Alexander Hamilton Ladd lived in it until his death in 1900. No one has called it home since; in 1913, the Society of Colonial Dames in New Hampshire leased (later to buy) the property and since have kept it open for guided tours during summer and early fall.

The Moffatt-Ladd House is as good an example as exists of how life was lived among the class that made up Portsmouth's de facto aristocracy during the late colonial and Federal periods, and the first years of the 19th century. (The Colonial Dames have concentrated on restoration and furnishing efforts—using pieces original to the house as they became available—upon the period of the Moffatt and early Ladd tenancies.) In the great entrance hall, hand-carved white pine woodwork is set off by Parisian wallpaper, imported in 1815, decorated with scenes of the Bay of Naples in subtle shades of gray. An upstairs chamber is curtained and its chairs upholstered in yellow damask. Persian carpets, porcelain from the Orient,

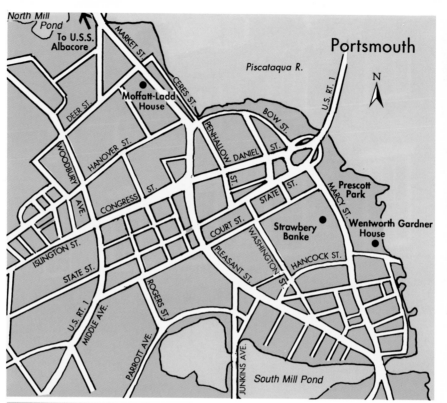

The halcyon years of Portsmouth's seagoing commerce, before the war of 1812, were the years when the great Federal-style mansions were built.

PATRICIA J. BRUNO

Built in Portsmouth, the U.S.S. Albacore once set submarine speed records. Now it has a fixed address, and is regularly boarded by inquisitive tourists.

9

parlor sets in the styles of Chippendale and Hepple-white—these were the household commonplaces of those Portsmouth generations who sent their ships to the corners of the earth.

The most telling of all the features of the Mof-fatt-Ladd House is a narrow parlor, extending along the front of the house for much of the second floor. Twelve leather-bottomed chairs, here at least since the inventory of 1768, stand spaced in a row facing the windows. These are the chairs at which the Mof-fatts and their colleagues in trade sat watching the Piscataqua and the harbor beyond, back when the phrase "waiting for your ship to come in" was not an idle cliche but a vital measure of a merchant's life. In those days, the view was clear; the house being built high enough that the upper floors afforded a line of sight above the roofs of warehouses across the lane. (One of those warehouses, the family's own, was con-nected to the house's basement by a tunnel; did Sam-uel Moffatt begin his flight to the islands by this sub-terranean route?) How many mornings and afternoons did the burghers of Portsmouth spend in this room, heated only by New England rum, talking Federalist politics and keeping an eye to the horizon? By con-trast, Alexander Hamilton Ladd's beautiful formal garden, a neatly hidden expanse of lawns, arbors and flower beds behind the house, seems like a place de-voted to turning away from the vigor of commerce, a retreat from the front lines of harbor-watching that paralleled Portsmouth's own near-retirement.

People do not come to Market Street in Portsmouth today to look for ships in the harbor—unless, perhaps, they are waiting for the Isles of Shoals cruise ship to come into its berth at Barker Wharf. Market Street today is still all business, but it is the business of antiques shops and boutiques, hall-marks of the city's post-1960s transformation. Where once-decrepit warehouses or dusty ship chandlers' shops dominated the waterfront and its adjacent streets, now the fashionable accoutrements of south-ern New Hampshire's white-collar economic boom have taken over. Ceres Street, a narrow alley that runs between the harbor and the backs of the buildings facing Market Street, is an examplar of the trend: in one short block, it contains two popular restaurants, a homemade ice cream emporium, and a well stocked small bookstore; at its head, on the corner of Bow Street, there are two more restaurants and an outdoor cafe.

Sometimes it seems as if restaurants have become Portsmouth's single most important industry, occupying at least as vital a position in the local economy as overseas trade once did. That may be overstating the situation a bit, but nevertheless it is easy to imagine that if the 12 leather chairs commanding the harbor at the Moffatt-Ladd House were to be occupied today, it would be by restaurateurs watching carloads of hungry out-of-towners come up Market Street from Route 95. I don't know who keeps track of such things, but I have heard from several sources that Portsmouth now has more restaurants per capita than any city in the United States.

Ceres Street is a good place to start if you have a mind to sample Portsmouth's restaurants: it's the home of owner/chef James Haller's Blue Strawbery, which may as well be given credit for having started Portsmouth's culinary rebirth back in 1970. Haller's menu, which draws on the best traditions of French provincial cookery and the inventive nontraditions of what has become known as "New American" cuisine, is served in a cozy ground-floor space carved from an ancient waterfront warehouse; the setting, too, was a harbinger of the way restaurants were going to look in restored seaport communities.

From Ceres Street, Portsmouth's gustatory horizons extend throughout the city in at least a half dozen ethnic directions: Tex-Mex at Poco Diablo and northern Italian at Guido's around the corner on Bow Street; Chinese at Szechuan Taste on Daniel Street and Japanese at Sakura on Pleasant Street, neither more than a few blocks away. For a touch of the old-time red-sauce religion, in an unpretentious bistro atmosphere that cheerfully predates just about everything hereabouts short of the Naval Shipyard, head for Rosa's, an Italian restaurant down on State Street. After all, chicken cacciatore and veal parme-

Above: Downtown Portsmouth, all brick and stone, and neat as a pin.
Left: The elegantly pilastered structure at the center of this block in Market Square is the Portsmouth Athenaeum, a private library dating from the early 1800s.
Facing page: The Moffatt-Ladd House, Portsmouth, as seen from its gardens. This was the world of Portsmouth's moneyed elite nearly two centuries ago.

PATRICIA J. BRUNO

Above: *The Dunaway Store, part of the collection of restored 17-, 18th- and 19th-century Portsmouth structures known as Strawbery Banke.*
Right: *The gardens behind Portsmouth author Thomas Bailey Aldrich's home at Strawbery Banke contain all of the flowers mentioned in his poetry.*
Facing page: *Part of the flower gardens at Strawbery Banke.*

ROBERT PERRON

san are irreducible elements in life—like the bricks and mortar of Portsmouth itself—that cannot be altered by the arrival on the scene of chic 1980s trattorias and sushi bars. Rosa's was here when this city had precious few restaurants per capita, and never had a clue that it was going for the record. Like the newsstands and tobacconists and old-fashioned jewelers that stand fast against the boutiquing of nearby Market Square, Rosa's is a window on an older Portsmouth, an older New England.

This end of State Street, in fact, reveals a general diminution of the buffed, post-restoration patina of the immediate downtown area. It shows in the bars—one place, probably a shore-leave hangout in years gone by, now has a clientele of bikers that can account for a string of 60 or 70 Harleys lining the curb on a Friday night (the bikers appear to be harmless, and to make sure that you are, too, a sentry watches over the bikes from a post near the saloon door)—and in a pair of used-book shops. The Book Guild, in particular, has a good range of antiquarian Portsmouthiana and New Hampshire and New England titles, as well as a broad selection of general non-fiction and fiction volumes. Here you might come across the work of Celia Thaxter, the 19th-century poet, salon-keeper and gardener who made her home on the Isles of Shoals; or a copy of the late 18th-century history of New Hampshire by Reverend Jeremy Belknap, the first thorough chronicler of the Granite State. Or, you may chance to pick up an old copy of Thomas Bailey Aldrich's *The Story of a Bad Boy*, a fictionalized account of the author's errant youth in a town called Rivermouth.

Rivermouth is, of course, Portsmouth, and the neighborhood in which Aldrich lived—in fact, the house where he spent his childhood—stands directly south of lower State Street. Now known as Strawbery Banke, after the original name of the settlement that became Portsmouth, this district of narrow streets and ancient houses represents a conscious, deliberate and systematic effort to preserve and interpret the city's past, as opposed to the patchwork of private and public, residential and commercial restoration that characterizes the rest of Portsmouth's streets and squares. In the late 1950s, the neighborhood was familiar to older Portsmouth residents as "Puddle Dock" after a long-since-filled tidal inlet once lined with commercial wharves. Its houses were in a sad state of disrepair, many of them having been occupied continuously since the 1700s by progressively poorer generations of owners and tenants. Puddle Dock was ripe for the 1950s remedy of choice for tired old neighborhoods, the wholesale bulldozing known as "urban renewal."

Fortunately, a coalition of citizens concerned about Portsmouth and its past succeeded in turning the plans for Puddle Dock around. Instead of tearing the old quarter down, they argued, why not restore its irreplaceable stock of buildings and open them to the public as a town-within-a-town? Thus the funds earmarked for demolition were redirected towards preservation, and the non-profit, private institution called Strawbery Banke came into being. Its charge is the ongoing restoration, management and interpretation of more than 40 structures on a 10-acre parcel tucked within the blocks formed by Court, Marcy, Hancock and Washington streets. A single admission charge allows visitors access to the entire property, and to as many of the houses as have been restored and furnished or fitted with educational exhibits.

Thomas Bailey Aldrich's boyhood home, which stands adjacent to a garden containing all of the flowers named in his poetry and a museum devoted to Aldrich manuscripts and memorabilia, was the first of Strawbery Banke's houses to be preserved; a memorial organization acquired it and furnished it with as much as could be found of the author's own belongings shortly after his death in 1907. Included among these association pieces is the table at which Aldrich wrote *The Story of A Bad Boy*.

Flanking the 1797 Aldrich House are two older Strawbery Banke structures, one whose past is largely private and another that figured as a public meeting place during the most tumultuous era in Portsmouth's history. The 1762 Chase House, on the corner of Court and Washington streets, was the home

Above: *The formal plantings at Prescott Park, on the Portsmouth waterfront opposite Strawbery Banke.*
Right: *Built in 1795, the Drisco House at Strawbery Banke has been restored to show both 18th- and 20th-century uses of the structure.*
Facing page: *Springtime at Prescott Park.*

of merchant prince Stephen Chase; his family occupied the mansion through the mid-1800s. It now is furnished to reflect the Federalist heyday, circa 1800. At Court and Atkinson streets, the 1766 Pitt Tavern stands as a reminder of the forces that divided Portsmouth as the American Revolution approached. For a while, Tory townsmen met here over cider and ale; later, the rebels who sent colonial governor John Wentworth packing made it their gathering place. Strawbery Banke maintains it today as a museum.

Not all of the occupants of the houses preserved at Strawbery Banke were famous, or even prominent. The 1780 Wheelwright House, at Jefferson Street and Horse Lane, was the home of a sea captain who never attained a life of wealth and ease—although pine paneling he likely took for granted would make his house an extremely desirable period piece were it on the market today, attracting buyers far more well off than Capt. Wheelwright ever was. Today, Strawbery Banke interpreters in 18th-century dress demonstrate the art of fireplace cookery at the captain's kitchen hearth. Sad to say, the insurance company doesn't allow them to offer samples to visitors.

Built in 1695, the Sherburne House facing Horse Lane is the oldest of Strawbery Banke's structures. Instead of attempting to return the house to its original appearance, though, Strawbery Banke's historians and craftsmen have opted to turn the old structure into an object lesson in the science and art of restoration. Cutaway views showing centuries of alteration, accompanied by displays explaining terms and methods, give a good sense of the detective work and sensitive reconstruction techniques involved in bringing an ancient piece of carpentry back to a semblance of its original state.

Crafts other than that of the housewright also are given their place at Strawbery Banke. A 1790 tenant house contains an exhibit of handmade textiles and the shop of a working weaver; another houses a pottery shop. At the 1810 residence of cooper Peter Lowd, a collection of 18th- and 19th-century hand tools is on exhibit.

Much to its credit, Strawbery Banke is not con-

cerned exclusively with the Colonial, Federalist and Victorian past. Given the large stock of housing and small commercial structures that the restoration's planners had to work with, the decision was made to focus also upon the lives and material surroundings of Puddle Dock residents during the earlier years of our own century.

The 1795 Drisco House, opposite the admission office on Puddle Lane (the house once faced the fetid waters of Puddle Dock), has been given a fascinating split personality. On the right side of the central hallway is a picture-perfect recreation of late-18th-century shopkeeper's rooms, with a store in front and family quarters in back. But look to the left, and you'll see a far more familiar sight: a working-class living room and kitchen typical of the early 1950s, a time when many of Strawbery Banke's colonial dwellings had long since been partitioned into small apartments. The rooms are authentic to the last detail—television, sofa, linoleum, small kitchen appliances; even the packaged foodstuffs and magazines are true to the era. It all makes good museum sense. After all, the blue-collar families who lived in Puddle Dock during the Eisenhower years led lives significantly removed from present-day circumstances, if not so dramatically different as those of the small tradesmen of Adams's and Jefferson's time.

At the Joshua Jackson House, an unretouched view of the cold-water–flat era is offered. Intended to show how a typical Strawbery Banke building looked prior to restoration, the Jackson House is a creaking hulk with its alligatored paint, peeling wallpaper and cracked plaster unretouched; at one point, the wall covering is peeled back to reveal a scrap of 1932 newspaper. The gray-carpeted walkway that guides visitors through the house, past photo-and-text displays telling about the family who lived here in the 1930s and 1940s, lends an eerie feeling to the place, as if we are aliens walking through a museum of life among the working poor in midcentury America. If these houses harbor any shades, the old-timers in knee breeches must be crowded by the citizens of

PATRICIA J. BRUNO

Depression-era Portsmouth, inhabitants of the now distant-seeming day before yesterday.

Thanks to a sound sense of historic preservation that extends to the privately-owned property along the streets outside the gates of Strawbery Banke, we can be reasonably assured that the Portsmouth of the day after tomorrow—at least in this part of town—will look much as it does today. One of the best ways to finish the ramble through waterfront Portsmouth—that began at the *Albacore* and the Moffatt-Ladd House—is to walk from the main entrance of Strawbery Banke through Prescott Park, which has beautifully-maintained formal flower gardens in spring, summer and early fall, and into the quiet neighborhood of neatly-restored wooden row houses that extends south of Hancock Street, between South Mill Pond and Little Harbor. The side streets are narrow, and the houses that line them were never at all pretentious; any skipper who lived here in the days of the tall ships couldn't have been doing even as well as old Captain Wheelwright. The current generation is probably the most prosperous that ever lived here. But the neighborhood has been gentrified quietly , and today stands as one of those quintessential habitations of coastal New England, an archetype like Marblehead or Newburyport in Massachusetts or the trim peninsular villages Down East along the Maine coast. It is a neighborhood that seems to look to sea, and its crowning glory, the Wentworth-Gardner House, stands at Gardner and Mechanic Streets so close to the water that it isn't hard to imagine a bowsprit rustling the second-floor window curtains.

Like the Moffatt-Ladd, the Wentworth-Gardner House was built as a gift, this time from Madame Mark Hunking Wentworth to her son Thomas in 1760. This house, too, is a prime piece of Georgian architecture, and in the opinion of some it is one of New England's best. Block-fronted and heavily quoined at the corners, it has a steeper pitch to its hipped roof than that of Moffatt-Ladd, and its front door is surmounted by a crest decorated with carved pineapples—colonial symbols of hospitality, as a pineapple was a rare and expensive treat to offer a guest. The little world behind those wooden fruits was as perfectly appointed as anything Portsmouth ever has seen, and this city obviously has known its share of opulence. (The interior woodcarving alone took more than a year for Madame Wentworth's artisans to complete.) Strangely enough, though, the house and all it contains once almost was dismantled and packed off to a city that has seen even more opulence and thrives on a steady diet of it. The Metropolitan Museum of Art once owned the Wentworth-Gardner House, and had plans to move it to Central Park. Foolish New Yorkers! They ought to have realized that the only place for a great house built by New England seafaring money is standing squarely on the banks of its harbor, forever looking for its ships to come in.

DAVID A. WHITE

Above: Portsmouth fishing docks, at dawn on a summer day.
Facing page: A scene at Strawbery Banke, suggesting that an 18th-century cooper has just gone off for his afternoon cider.

2 Exeter to Durham
Canoeing Great Bay

The sign on the Portsmouth shop door said "Nautical Charts," so I went in and asked for 13285, Portsmouth to Dover and Exeter—the chart taking in the whole of Great Bay. "Where's Great Bay?" the clerk asked.

Great Bay is the largest inland body of salt water in New England, and its eastern shores are less than five miles from where we were standing. My immediate reaction was to lament the decline of geographic knowledge on even the most immediate local level—never mind where Baffin Island or the Serengeti Plain is—but on the way home, it occurred to me that very few people, even in southern New Hampshire, ever see Great Bay unless they live on it. With the exception of state Route 4, which runs briefly along a northern arm called Little Bay, no public roads of any importance pass near this shallow, landlocked tidal sea. Great Bay begins as an appendage of the Piscataqua River and swells south for five miles through the towns of Newington, Greenland, Stratham, Durham, Newmarket and Newfields until it is nearly three and a half miles across during high tide at its widest point. Part of it is bordered by Pease Air Force Base, strictly off limits to civilians, and the rest is largely rimmed round by private landholdings. Only by hiking out to the eastern tip of the Adams Point State Wildlife Management Area in Durham can you come to any publicly accessible perspective of the bay. So, I forgave the clerk her ignorance of Great Bay. Out of sight, out of mind.

Actually, this was why I was buying the nautical chart. If I wanted to see Great Bay—a body of water that was hidden in plain view, like Poe's purloined letter—it made sense to forget the highways and even the back roads, and to make my approach by water.

There are certainly enough ways to do it. In addition to the Piscataqua, whose tidal action contributes to the bay's salinity, Great Bay is fed by the Bellamy, Oyster, Lamprey and Squamscott Rivers, and by a number of meandering creeks. My plan was to launch a canoe on one of the southern tributaries

at high tide, paddle north into the bay proper, and then follow one of the northern feeder steams to its source, preferably late enough in the day so that the tide already would have receded and now would be advancing inland again.

The choice of canoe put-in and take-out points was easy. Of the rivers that flow into Great Bay, one whose source is farthest south is the Squamscott River. Rising as a freshwater stream near Raymond, some 15 miles farther inland, it becomes a tidal river at the falls and mill dam in downtown Exeter and then twists northward for just short of six miles to meet the bay. As for the other end of the trip, the alternatives narrowed down to the Oyster River leading northwest into Durham. The Piscataqua itself is a fast river, with strong currents, and the Bellamy ends up paralleling an expressway on its way up to Dover. Durham is a pleasant little town with a handy public landing, right at the end of the Oyster River's tidal portion. From Exeter to Durham via Great Bay, the trip would cover a shade over 14 miles.

Exeter was one of New Hampshire's earliest settlements; only Portsmouth and Dover are older. The Reverend John Wheelwright, a dissenter from the Puritan orthodoxy of Boston, came here in 1638 and negotiated a deed for the surrounding territory from the sagamore of the Squamscott tribe, Wehanownowit. He was joined by only a handful of co-religionists at first, but by 1642 the town had grown sufficiently large to assume equal footing with its two predecessors. Over the course of the 17th and 18th centuries, Exeter grew to be politically important (throughout most of the American Revolution, it was the capital of New Hampshire) and prosperous, with much of the local industry dependent upon the power provided by the Squamscott Falls. By 1800 there were grist, saw- and paper mills, as well as factories producing goods as diverse as snuff, chocolate and cotton cloth. Exeter's last two centuries, though,

Facing page: *The northern reaches of Great Bay, as seen from Durham.*

have seen the water-powered mills along the Squamscott fall silent, and a much more famous enterprise rise to prominence. The town is the home of Phillips Exeter Academy, founded in 1783 by John Phillips, a successful Exeter merchant who had five years earlier established the other Phillips Academy in his native Andover, Massachusetts. Today Phillips Exeter is one of America's most prestigious college preparatory schools. It occupies a spacious campus along Exeter's Front Street, uphill from the river, with many buildings designed by the master of colonial-revival architecture, New Hampshire native Ralph Adams Cram.

In a sense, this canoe trip from Exeter to Durham by way of Great Bay is a trip from prep school to college. Durham is the home of the University of New Hampshire, the state's principal public institution of higher learning. The university started life as a state agricultural college in Hanover, but moved to Durham in 1893 when a rich farmer's legacy became available on condition that the school be transplanted here, to the site of his farm. Modern-day UNH, though, is more devoted to the liberal arts than to agriculture.

As with Hanover and Exeter, Durham's history as a town often tends to be obscured by its stature as an academic center. But here, too, is a settlement that goes back a lot farther than the school within its boundaries. Durham's first colonists came from Dover, sailing into the Oyster River via the Piscataqua and the upper reaches of Great Bay (or Little Bay, as its narrow northern arm is called). They found the elbow room they were looking for, but they paid for it with the vulnerability to Indian attacks characteristic of outlying communities in the late 17th and early 18th centuries. A 1675 raid on Durham marked the opening of hostilities in King Philip's War, while the 1694 sacking and burning of the town ranked as one of the worst atrocities of the era of French-English hostility. This attack was carried out by Indians, but it was planned in Quebec and led by a French soldier. More than 100 Durham residents were killed or taken captive, and most of

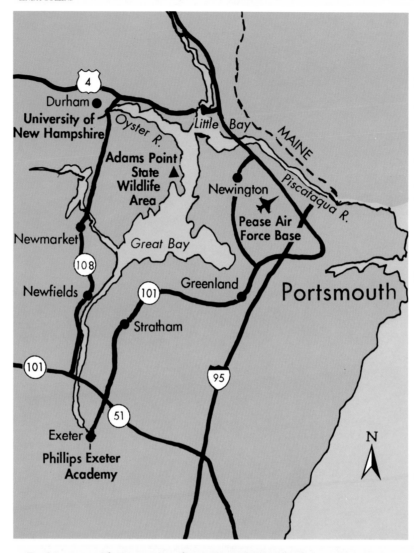

Two hundred years ago, Exeter was a seaport, with shipbuilding and a trade that extended as far as the West Indies.

Facing page: *The University of New Hampshire at Durham. Originally an agricultural college, UNH now offers a wide variety of undergraduate and graduate programs in liberal arts and the sciences.*

the town was reduced to ashes. To see the peaceful little college town come into view from the river today is to realize just what an eternity 300 years is, especially in North American time.

But we still have a good way to go to get to the Oyster River. I started this trip, with my canoeing partner Mike Hoel, at the Exeter town boat launch on Water Street. High tide, fortunately enough, synchronized with an appropriate hour for beginning a 14-mile paddle: at seven in the morning, there was plenty of water in the Squamscott below the falls. We put the boat in the water and started downstream, with the old brick mills to our right and town streets directly on our left quickly disappearing in favor of clumps of freshwater cordgrass. The idea of leaving town for open water had a mock-heroic feeling about it, considering the size of the town and the size of the boat, but we recalled that 200 years ago, Exeter really was a seaport, with a trade that extended as far as the West Indies. There were shipbuilding yards here, too, turning out commercial vessels as well as frigates of war. The Squamscott and Great Bay were their avenue to Portsmouth and the North Atlantic. What a figure those tall ships must have cut, gliding through these marshes toward the sea!

We couldn't feel as if we were entirely away into the country until we put well behind us the sounds of four-lane Route 101, which crosses the Squamscott at a height that would have clipped the masts off a frigate. But at that point there still was plenty of river left, winding between the rural towns of Stratham and Newfields. The Squamscott flows for almost six miles from Exeter to Great Bay, and as it broadens and slows along this distance there is ample opportunity to observe the gradual changes that mark the transition from freshwater to brackish to saltwater riverine environment—for example, the thinning of the cordgrass and its replacement with *spartina altiflora*, a mainstay grass of the true salt marsh. These telltale signs don't occur abruptly, just as salt water doesn't abruptly replace fresh in an estuary like the Squamscott. Instead it is a subtle equation in which the strength of the river's current is balanced against that of the incoming tides: the outward push of Rockingham County's brooks and freshets on one side, and the inward rush of the moon-drawn Atlantic on the other.

We were pleased to see a good number of birds. Black ducks—much less common now in New England than mallards—broke from the water as we rounded several marshy points; we also passed a pair of mergansers and saw sleek cormorants stand with wings arched to dry their feathers. The real surprise, though, was the number of great blue herons along the shore. We counted seven or eight herons, all of them stalking the muddy banks with their peculiar, hesitant, gangly-legged walk. Invariably they would be spooked by the silent but incongruous canoe, and would go into that loose-jointed heron takeoff that seems such an unlikely prelude to graceful flight.

North of Newfields, things began to look decidedly nautical on the Squamscott; there are little fishing boats at anchor, and here and there a stack of lobster pots in a back yard. Just beyond an old Boston and Maine Railroad bridge in fixed position low above the water (the reason there are no sailboats upstream), the Squamscott finally opened into Great Bay. Here was the revelation we had come for, what neither of us ever had seen during the decades we had lived fewer than 20 miles away. Here was great calm expanse of water, perhaps 10 square miles in all if anyone cared to measure its wildly irregular contours. Great Bay is shaped very roughly like one of those ship's decanters, fat and wide at the bottom with a long, arrow neck. Entering as we did near the decanter's bottom, nearly every shore seemed far away, and only occasionally were there houses among the bordering trees. But for all its breadth and blueness, Great Bay has little volume except in its central channel. The estuary is so shallow that low-tide readings on the nautical chart are a half foot in places, and many stretches between the shoreline and the channel are given no soundings at all. Those early sailors and shipbuilders had to know their tides well, even in the days when there was less silt on the river bottoms. No wonder that Great Bay and its tributar-

ANN REID

DAVID A. WHITE

Above: *A weir on the Lamprey River, Newmarket. The Indians caught fish by means of weirs long before white men settled New Hampshire; today, the traps are limited to locations where weir fishing was practiced before restrictive legislation went into effect.*
Left: *A great blue heron stalks the shallows on Great Bay.*
Facing page: *Almost entirely surrounded by land, the waters of Great Bay offer a fine, protected environment for sailing and windsurfing. Tides are extreme, though, and this morning's inlet is liable to be this afternoon's mud flat.*

23

ies were once the realm of a remarkable craft called the gundalow.

The gundalows, or "Piscataqua gundalows" as they were called locally, were broad, flat-bottomed boats described as resembling the shallow wood kneading troughs common in country kitchens. Some smaller, earlier models had open hulls, while later a flat deck came into use. A gundalow could be poled along, or it could be rigged quickly with a lateen sail affixed to a yard that swung flat against the deck. These homely but practical boats shipped country goods—notably salt hay, cordwood and farm produce—to Portsmouth, and brought imports and manufactured items (and later coal) to the upriver communities. Before 1850, there was even a scheduled gundalow packet service between Portsmouth and Newmarket by way of the Lamprey River, past whose mouth we paddled soon after entering Great Bay. Eventually, though, the railroad reached every inland town that mattered, and by 1900 gundalows were obsolete. But they were enough of a part of southern New Hampshire's folk heritage for an outfit called the Portsmouth Gundalow Project to launch a faithful replica in 1982. It can be seen, when it is not off touring the backwaters, at its home port near Portsmouth's Strawbery Banke restoration.

As we crossed Great Bay from south to north, we witnessed two remarkably different flight displays. The first came courtesy of the U.S. Air Force and its trainers, fighters and lumbering transports; Pease AFB is a busy place, and anyone who sails or canoes Great Bay has to pay for the silent stretches by putting up with the occasional roar of jet engines. I thought it would bother me more than it did, but in fact very little time elapses between the first sighting of a fighter and its landing beyond the trees to starboard, in a puff of black exhaust.

The other fliers we encountered at mid-bay were far more numerous than Pease's jets, and far more attuned to our own progress on the water. As we made our way northward, just beyond the widest part of Great Bay, we saw a flock of at least 300 Canada geese settled on the surface in a vast, spread-out

DAVID A. WHITE

ANN REID PHOTO COURTESY OF SEA GRANT EXTENSION PROGRAM, UNIVERSITY OF NEW HAMPSHIRE

formation, like ships of the line. We had several hundred yards to cover before we would get anywhere near them, and we expected that long before our own close approach they would be startled into flight by a pair of power boats moving behind them, along the opposite shore. But the power boats came and went, and the geese of the line still straddled the bay before us. The closer we paddled, the longer their array seemed to be. At 200 yards we could hear their agitation, and we knew that it would be an intrusive green canoe that would drive the geese off the water.

Suddenly, with a great commotion of wingbeats, the birds left the water, their line breaking at a point directly ahead as they flew toward us and off to either side. Geese to port, geese to starboard, and the wonderful cacophony of good music in living stereo: simply by plying our paddles in silent approach we had occasioned this elemental display. If two F-16s from Pease had thundered towards us and split formation overhead, it would have been only noisier, but no more impressive.

Furber Strait is the neck of the Great Bay decanter, its approach marked on the west by the tiny Footman Islands and the hilly protrusion of Adams Point. Named for the Adams family, 18th- and 19th-century owners of this corner of Durham who once were active in the gundalow trade, Adams Point is today one of the few parcels of public land along the shores of Great Bay. Its 61 acres of open land and forest, laced with trails and old stone walls, comprise the Adams Point Wildlife Management Area, maintained by the New Hampshire Fish and Game Department.

Adams Point is accessible via a road across the tidal marshes crowding the narrow neck that connects it with the mainland, and this is how most people arrive for an afternoon of birding or walking the shoreline and interior trails. The point seemed made for an approach by canoe, though, and we found a quiet cove in which to beach our boat and have lunch. Afterwards, a brief exploration on foot revealed a microcosm of southern New Hampshire: tracts of second-growth woodland, at one time fields

DAVID A. WHITE

Above: Canoeists on the Squamscott River, part of the Great Bay estuarine system. These paddlers have gathered as part of a celebration of Coast Month, initiated to increase awareness of the importance and fragility of coastal ecosystems.
Left: Morning on Great Bay, before the sun burns off the haze.
Facing page: Two vessels of the inshore fishing fleet at anchor along the lower reaches of the Squamscott River, near Great Bay. So long as they remain healthy, estuaries such as the bay are vital parts of the marine food chain upon which commercial fishermen depend.

25

Above: A farmhouse at Brentwood, just west of Exeter. Dark colors, we are told, absorb more heat—but how could New England be New England without its white houses and churches?
Right: A pair of Canada geese, during nesting season on the perimeter of Great Bay.
Facing page: Exeter celebrates its 350th anniversary. The founders, no doubt, would have looked upon fireworks as a wasteful extravagance—if not as a direct manifestation of collusion with dark powers.

farmed by generations of Adamses; weedy meadows in the sere shades of autumn; rocky beaches facing open water and tranquil mudflats (just reappearing as the tide began to slacken) closer to the western shore. Near the center of the peninsula, the only sign of a long history of human habitation was the Adams cenotaph, a white marble obelisk marking the grave-sites of family members. The oldest name on the stone was that of Reformation John Adams (1791-1850), a throwback to the great age of Puritan nomenclature that gave us such first names as "Hate-Evil" and "Search-the-Scriptures." We suspect that "John" was what they called R. J. Adams.

The Adamses and other early settlers used their position on the shores of Great Bay to advantage in fishing, oyster-harvesting and water-borne commerce. The people who work here today, however, follow a pursuit that benefits the bay and its creatures as much as it does humankind. Just around the cove from where we beached our canoe stands the Jackson Estuarine Laboratory (JEL), a branch of the University of New Hampshire's Institute of Marine Science and Ocean Engineering. The JEL's twofold mission of education and research centers upon the unique characteristics of the estuarine environment—a natural system in which the intermingling of salt and fresh water nurtures one of the most diverse biotic communities on earth.

Estuaries like Great Bay are not only phenomenally productive, with a majority of our commercial fish and shellfish species dependent on estuarine food chains at various times in their life cycles; they are fragile, and all too susceptible to disruption of their delicate biological balance as the result of pollution and overdevelopment of adjacent lands. Understandably, much of the research done by JEL scientists concentrates upon threats to the well-being of estuaries: acid rain, ocean waste disposal, effects of pollution on bottom-dwelling animals, and the extent to which the environment can or cannot absorb heavy metal and organic pollutants. In addition to the laboratory itself, with its marine-organism incubation chambers and specimen tanks fed by a constant flow of estuary water, the JEL maintains two research vessels and a fishing boat for work involving nets and shellfish cultivation.

Great Bay narrows considerably north of Adams Point; in fact, from here to the Oyster River it is technically known as Little Bay in view of its less than one-mile width. Two miles of travel beyond the laboratory brought us to Durham Point, where we left the bay behind to turn westward and paddle the last two and a half miles upriver to our take-out point at Durham. The Oyster River's banks are more built-up than those of the Squamscott or of Great Bay itself, and we saw at least a half-dozen houses that were either brand new or still under construction. If the terrain of Adams Point had mirrored southern New Hampshire's natural environment, here was a summation of trends in human settlement in this part of the Granite State. The counties bordering Massachusetts are in the midst of an economic boom, and the building permit is its certificate of validation. Not that the banks of the Oyster River resemble the denser parts of New Jersey; this is still a semirural area. But it is semirural on the way to being suburban, if present trends continue. Should that be the case, we will be thankful for whatever the UNH researchers can tell us about how best to deal and not deal with a living estuary—assuming, of course, that such knowledge can inspire protective laws. New Hampshire, with its grand tradition of laissez-faire, has not exactly led the world in the field of progressive environmental legislation.

All it takes is a canoe trip from Exeter to Durham, in the company of herons and geese, to bring such thoughts to mind.

Manchester
Industrial Revolution Cradle

3

There are other cities that can lay claim to the title of cradle of the industrial revolution in America. Lowell, Massachusetts, was set to spinning and weaving by a syndicate of Boston investors in 1817. Paterson, New Jersey was planned as the new nation's first industrial city in the early 1790s, although it didn't really make its name in silk and locomotives until several decades afterward. But neither Lowell nor Paterson, nor any American city, ever spawned anything quite like the Amoskeag Manufacturing Company. If, for better or worse, bigness and vertical integration have become the hallmarks of American industry, then it can truly be said that Manchester was the town and Amoskeag the enterprise that set the standard for the way we make things.

Judge Samuel Blodgett stood at the Amoskeag Falls one day in 1810, and said of the surrounding village—it was called Derryfield in those days—that this would be "the Manchester of New England." Blodgett was a likely character to predict that the town built along the river would someday rival the British textile manufacturing center. He had spent a good part of his life promoting the idea of a canal around the Amoskeag Falls of the Merrimack, and had seen his dream become reality in 1807. With the new water link with Boston by way of the Middlesex Canal, and a ready supply of power right at the falls, Derryfield could begin to realize its destiny as a manufacturing center.

The first entrepreneur to open a textile mill at Derryfield (it would change its name to Manchester in 1810) was Benjamin Prichard, who used the energy of the swift-flowing Merrimack to spin cotton starting in 1805. Within a few years the factory came to be called Amoskeag, after the falls.

In those early years, weavers still worked at home, on hand looms. It wasn't until 1819, when power looms came into use, that all of the work from spinning raw cotton fiber to finishing fabric was brought under the factory roof. The new integrated system was not a financial success, however. The business was sold in 1822, and reorganized nine years later as the Amoskeag Manufacturing Company by the same group of Boston capitalists who had begun building Lowell into a textile center. With $1 million in capital, the Boston men began to look beyond the immediate business of spindles and looms. They bought water power rights to the entire Merrimack River, and assembled a parcel of 15,000 acres on the Merrimack's east bank near the falls. Starting in 1837, they laid out and built the city of Manchester.

Manchester and "the Amoskeag," as it was always called, grew up together from that moment on. The company auctioned off building lots to developers of housing and retail blocks, and donated the land on which municipal institutions—including Manchester's City Hall—would be built. The mill operations grew even more extensive, as the directors expanded manufacturing space along the river and bought out much of their competition. The end result, at its pinnacle of size and power in the early years of the 20th century, was a giant enterprise that employed as many as to 17,000 workers to tend its 700,000 spindles and 23,000 looms. The Amoskeag ran its own hydroelectric generating station, in the years after direct use of water power became obsolete, and operated its own machine shops for the manufacture and repair of textile-making equipment (a little-known aspect of the company's history is that as an outgrowth of its machinery sideline, it built and sold more than 200 locomotives between 1849 and 1856). The railroad spur lines that served the mill complex along the east bank of the Merrimack were constantly busy with unloading raw cotton (and, to a much smaller extent, wool), and shipping the yard goods that were turned out at a rate of as much as a mile a minute, as well as with receiving the 150,000 tons of coal the company bought each year to supplement the energy derived from its hydro plant.

Facing page: One of the surviving structures of the Amoskeag mill complex, Manchester. A century ago, Amoskeag was the largest producer of cotton cloth in the world.

Manchester, meanwhile, grew to become a city of more than 50,000 people by the turn of the century. Although not all of those employed worked for the Amoskeag, it has been estimated that as much as two thirds of Manchester's jobs were dependent upon the textile giant and its related operations, and upon a service sector that existed primarily because of the circulation of Amoskeag wages in the community. Any outside enterprise that might want to set up shop in Manchester did so only at the pleasure of the Amoskeag, which owned the remaining acreage available for industrial development.

As Manchester's economy was determined by the Amoskeag, so was its social fabric. By the early 1900s this was largely an immigrant city. All of the European nationalities that flocked to the United States during the wide-open years of immigration were represented, but the predominant group in Manchester was French-Canadian. This was not mere happenstance, but was in large part the result of a concerted effort on the part of Amoskeag management to recruit Quebecois workers, particularly those from depressed rural areas. Quebec newspapers carried advertisements extolling the working conditions in the Manchester mills, and thousands of French-Canadians packed up their families and headed south on the Boston and Maine Railroad to heed the call.

French, Polish, Greek, Scottish or native Yankee, the millhands of the Amoskeag were part of as paternalistic a system of employment as ever existed in the United States, with the possible exception of wholly-owned corporate towns such as the sleeping-car manufacturing center of Pullman, Illinois. Only a small fraction of the workers actually lived in company-owned housing, but the presence of the Amoskeag was nevertheless all-pervasive both before and after the factory whistles blew. The company sponsored clubs and sports teams, published a magazine, and ran night schools that offered English as a second language.

There was an Amoskeag playground for workers' children, a dental plan (during the company's later years), and even a mortgage assistance program for employees who wished to buy their own houses. All of this largesse was, of course, largely a matter of corporate self-interest. A principal objective was to keep organized labor out of the mills. Toward the same end, the Amoskeag maintained employee dossiers that recorded such transgressions as union organizing or anti-capital agitation.

While strikers in 1919, 1922, 1933 and 1934 were part of the combination of forces that led to the Amoskeag's demise, the picture was more complicated than the mere fact of labor unrest—prompted in large part by a 1922 wage cut coupled with an increase in work hours—would suggest. The 1920s was an era in which the base of the American textile industry was shifting to the South, where physical plants were newer and labor was cheaper. The Amoskeag's directors saw the new trend and rode with it, transferring a large part of its liquid assets to a holding company and ceasing to re-invest capital in the Manchester plant. The sheer volume of production capacity in the vast brick mills along the Merrimack had become more of a liability than an asset. The Amoskeag shut its doors in 1935, and its property was liquidated in bankruptcy proceedings the following year.

The history of Manchester over the past half century largely has been the story of a city's attempts—ultimately successful—to fill the void left by the departure of such a giant. Some three quarters of the Amoskeag mill buildings still are standing, and the efforts that have gone into making them productive once again mirror the struggle of urban New England to re-invent the concept of industry in the late 20th century. Some of the old mills are still derelict, or are occupied by marginal operations—but a core of three millyard buildings totaling more than a half million square feet of floor space have been revitalized as electronics company headquarters, advertising offices and even a television studio.

Any visitor's approach to Manchester should rightly begin where the city itself did, on the banks of the Merrimack River at the place the Indians

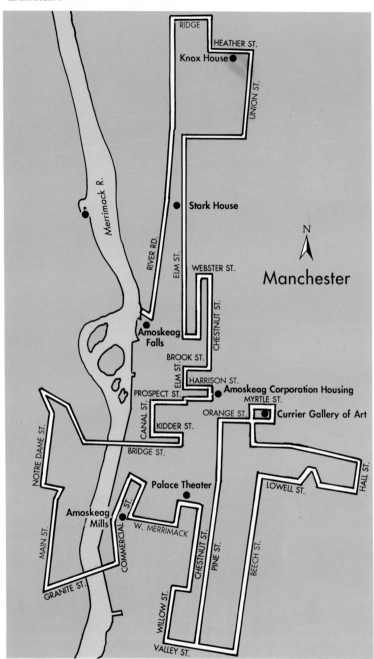

Any visitor's approach to Manchester should rightly begin where the city itself did, on the banks of the Merrimack River at the place the Indians called Amoskeag—"place of good fishing."

Facing page: *The Millyard, Manchester. When the Amoskeag Manufacturing Company was in business, thousands of workers swarmed through these doors each day.*

NONA BAUER

Above: *Statue of General John Stark, hero of the Revolution, in his native Manchester. Rallying his troops before the Battle of Bennington, Stark swore that victory would be theirs "or Molly Stark is a widow tonight!" It was, and she wasn't.*
Right: *Home of General John Stark, Manchester.*
Facing page: *Manchester's Victory Park.*

LAUNA ERNE

called Amoskeag—"place of good fishing." The location of the present Amoskeag Bridge, at Canal and West Salmon streets, is approximately at the site. Near here are the Amoskeag Falls, obscured now by a power dam, and the remains of the stone gatehouse that marked the place where Judge Samuel Blodgett's 1807 canal joined the Merrimack. The only physical evidence of the canal today is the stonework just downriver from the gatehouse of the modern power dam. This now-insignificant ruin is, like the later Amoskeag mill buildings, a tangible reminder of the forces that put Manchester on the map. Before the railroad came, several decades later, the Blodgett Canal was the town's commercial outlet to the world.

On the west bank of the river, opposite the power dam and falls, stood the earliest water-powered mills of what was called, at the beginning of the 19th century, "Amoskeag village." (The earlier town of Derryfield was centered farther east, in what is now the city's south side closer to Interstate 93 than to the river.) The original mill buildings were wooden, and no trace of them remains; today, a hotel and the hydro dam's power transformers occupy this site.

When the present Amoskeag Bridge was built in 1970, the work necessitated moving one of the oldest local structures, the Stark house. Built by Archibald Stark in 1737 at the east end of the Amoskeag Falls, this was the boyhood home of his son, General John Stark, hero of the Battle of Bennington in the American Revolution. The house now is located on Elm Street north of this site (one block east on West Salmon Street, then five blocks north of Elm to Waldo Street), and is maintained by the Daughters of the American Revolution. Its furnishings reflect the domestic styles of the Revolutionary War era—an era Stark well outlived. He died in Manchester in 1822, aged 93. He was by then the last of the generals of the Revolution, except for the Marquis de Lafayette.

The millyard and central concentration of brick factory buildings of the later Amoskeag Manufacturing Company stand about 15 blocks south of the falls and bridge. (Note: Manchester covers several miles of north-south distance along the Merrimack, and consequently no attempt will be made to recommend specific walking directions in these pages.) The first mill buildings on this side of the river were built in 1838; those that followed, through the 19th century, were constructed in uniform style of brick manufactured to be compatible in color and texture with that used in the existing mills. The resulting effect was of a visually harmonious city-within-a-city, clustered about the millyard; and despite the subsequent demolition of a quarter of the Amoskeag buildings—including those that once lined the narrow canals, also gone now—and the varied uses to which the surviving structures have been put, that effect largely remains.

At the south end of the millyard and along the east end of Canal Street are several rows of "Corporation Housing," as the Amoskeag's company-owned workers' tenements were called. Built between 1838 and 1914, the Corporation houses were never home to more than a fifth of the company's work force (except, perhaps, in the earliest years, when they served as dormitories for the "mill girls" recruited from New England farms in the days before immigrant labor), but were highly desirable as their rents were lower than Manchester's market rate. There was always a waiting list for occupancy, which was limited to large families having more than one member in the company's employ.

The Manchester Historic Association offers tours, each spring and fall, of the millyard and the remaining adjacent Amoskeag structures. The Association's headquarters—at which there are continuing and temporary exhibits relating to the city's past—are located at 129 Amherst Street, across from the Manchester Public Library.

Turn-of-the-century Manchester wasn't all work and no play, as is apparent from the history of the Palace Theater. The Palace, which stands on Hanover Street near the main downtown shopping thoroughfare of Elm Street, was built in 1915 by Victor Charas, a Greek immigrant who had made his

LAUNA ERNE

fortune as a restaurateur and speculator. The Manchester of Charas' day had an insatiable appetite for live entertainment: within the neighborhood of Hanover, Amherst, and Elm streets were nearly two dozen vaudeville and burlesque houses. It was Charas' objective to book the best vaudeville, and the best traveling repertory and Broadway show companies and, with confidence in the demand for high-quality productions, he built the Palace to seat more than 960 patrons, all of whom would have unobstructed views of a stage larger than those in most of the big New York theaters. In the summer, they enjoyed a primitive but effective air-conditioning system built around a vast block of ice and an immense fan in the basement.

The era of live performances at the Palace lasted until the 1930s, after which the big old theater passed several decades as a movie house. By the 1960s, it had sunk to X-rated ignominy. After several years during which it was leased for non-theatrical uses, the Palace was saved from demolition by a citizens' group called the New Hampshire Performing Arts Center, who set up a trust to restore the building and bring high-quality entertainment back to Hanover Street. The trust hadn't set itself an easy task, but after nearly two decades of upgrading the Palace's physical plant and rehabilitating its image with first-rate bookings, the theater shines as one of the brightest cultural lights in New Hampshire. Victor Charas' showplace is the home of the Manchester Chorale Society, the New Hampshire Symphony Orchestra and the New Hampshire Opera League, and serves as a venue for visiting dance, drama, musical and comedy troupes. If you're visiting the Manchester area for more than a day, find out what's playing and go—or at least stop by when the box office is open and take a look at the beautifully restored interior, one of the finest enclosed spaces in northern New England.

Manchester's most important cultural attraction is unquestionably the Currier Gallery of Art, at 192 Orange Street—six blocks east of Elm Street. Built in 1929 with a bequest from the estate of New

Hampshire Governor Moody Currier's widow, the Currier Gallery houses what is arguably the finest art collection in New England outside the Boston-Cambridge area. Here are European paintings, sculptures and decorative art of the past six centuries, as well as an impressive American collection. The galleries occupy two floors surrounding a central court, as well as a basement level; in addition, attached first-floor pavilions are devoted to 20th-century painting and sculpture, and to special exhibitions. The first-floor West Gallery houses European painting and sculpture, including Ian de Bray's *Banquet of Anthony and Cleopatra*, Tiepolo's *Triumph of Hercules*, Monet's *The Seine at Bougival* and *Cliffs at Etretat*, Picasso's *Woman Seated in a Chair*, and Rouault's *The Wounded Clown*. The second floor is exclusively American, with the exception of a tapestry gallery. Holdings include paintings by John Singer Sargent, Edward Hopper, Frederick Remington, Joseph Albers and Lyonel Feininger, as well as a 19th-century furniture collection that ranges from anonymous country pieces to the works of the Dunlop family, master cabinetmakers of late 18th-century New Hampshire.

A basement-level gallery houses contemporary American art, including works by Jasper Johns and George Bellows and photographs by the German émigré Lotte Jacobi, who settled in New Hampshire.

Manchester worked so long and so hard at earning the distinction of having the largest cotton textile mill in the world that it is ironic to think of it today in terms of boasting the best art museum in northern New England. But no one is complaining: the life that was the Amoskeag played out its century-long string of days, and left in its aftermath an economy and a society that were not only salvageable but also much the better for the diversity discovered.

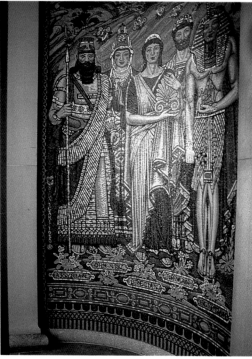

Above and left: *The Currier Gallery of Art, Manchester, houses New England's finest collection of painting and sculpture outside the greater Boston area.*
Facing page: *These solid brick Manchester rowhouses were part of the Amoskeag Corporation's "Corporation Housing" for workers with families. There was, of course, a considerable waiting list.*

GEORGE WUERTHNER

Concord
Capital Walking Tour

4

Above: Statue of Franklin Pierce, the only U.S. president born in New Hampshire, stands before the State Capitol in Concord. Pierce was once a legislator, lawyer and newspaperman here.
Facing page: New Hampshire's state capitol.

With a population of just above 30,000, Concord is a study in the small town as state capital. On these days of the southern New Hampshire high-tech boom, of course, Concord is pressing against its borders and spreading out into the suburbs, and it may well eventually creep far enough south along the Merrimack River and the Everett Turnpike to bump up against Manchester. But central Concord, the town that has collected along State and Main streets on the west bank of the river, comes across to the visitor as little more than an upcountry village big enough to sprout brick buildings. Brick buildings, and one big granite one with a proud golden dome.

Concord was among the earlier inland settlements of colonial New Hampshire. It was founded in 1659 as the Plantation of Pennycook, or Pennacook, a grant made by the Massachusetts Bay Company authorities to a group that included Major Richard Waldron, the Dover magistrate killed in the infamous 1689 Indian raid on that settlement. "Pennacook" was an Indian word meaning "crooked place," after the twisting course the Merrimack follows here.

Neither Waldron nor many other seacoast colonists cared to relocate at Pennacook during the first six decades after its technical founding. As New Hampshire remained under Massachusetts sovereignty, the Bay Colony re-granted the land on which Concord was to be built to another syndicate of settlers in 1725. Within two years, newcomers began to carve out their holdings along the "crooked place" on the Merrimack. Concord's Main Street was laid out in 1735, two years after the Massachusetts General Court chartered the town as Rumford. In 1765 New Hampshire—now an autonomous colony on equal footing with Massachusetts as part of British North America—rechartered the settlement as Concord.

The name "Rumford" may have been erased long ago from the town that was to become New Hampshire's capital, but it had been perpetuated in the noble title of one of the state's most illustrious colonial citizens. Benjamin Thompson, a Concord schoolteacher originally from Massachusetts, was an accomplished mathematician and scientist who performed valuable research on the transmission of heat. A fervent Tory, he left New Hampshire in 1774 and settled in England and, later, in Bavaria. When in 1791 the Elector of Bavaria named him a Count of the Holy Roman Empire, he chose the title "Count Rumford" after the older name of his erstwhile home. The term "Rumford fireplace," denoting a shallow, slope-backed hearth with good heat-deflecting abilities, dates back to the count's publication of his theories of fireplace design.

By the beginning of the 19th century, Concord had grown into a prosperous market town and center of a fledgling granite quarrying industry that was to make the town's name famous wherever American public buildings were erected during the expansive era that was to follow. The early years of the new century saw two developments that did more than anything else to boost Concord's importance: in 1808, an act of the state legislature moved New Hampshire's capital from Portsmouth to Concord. And just seven years later, the Middlesex Canal was completed, affording the town a direct, fully navigable water route to Boston. With the rapids at Amoskeag (Manchester) circumvented by the canal's locks, only one day was required to take laden barges downstream from Concord to Boston, and five days to bring them back up. Suddenly, seacoast granite from Rockport and Quincy had competition from the interior.

Concord is a town easily mastered by a visitor who prefers to do his or her sightseeing on foot. A good place to start is at the Eagle Hotel, on North Main Street directly opposite the State House Plaza. Built in 1852 on the site of a popular gathering place called the Eagle Coffee House, the Eagle Hotel became such a home-away-from-home for New Hampshire state legislators that it eventually became known as the "little State House." Sad to say, it is a hotel no longer; this is partly because people visiting towns the size of Concord nowadays prefer to stay in motels on the outskirts, and partly because highway

LAUNA ERNE

access to most of New Hampshire is now so good that the legislature doesn't really need a dormitory as much as it once did. The old hotel is now the focal point of an office-retail complex called Eagle Square Marketplace. (Another component, the Stone Warehouse and its adjacent one-time stable, is behind the hotel on the other side of Eagle Square.) At the hotel's enclosed central courtyard, you can pick up a brochure outlining the "Coach and Eagle Trail" connecting downtown's historic sites.

The first and foremost of these sites is, of course, the New Hampshire State House, which stands at the rear of the plaza bordered by North Main, Capitol, Park and North State streets. Built of Concord granite hewn by state prison inmates and dedicated in 1819, this is the oldest state capitol in the United States in which a legislature still meets in its original chambers. That "original chambers" qualification enables Concord boosters to finesse the question of Massachusetts, whose Bulfinch-designed state house is nearly a quarter-century older but whose legislature meets in an addition constructed in the late 1800s.

In any event, it's a good thing the Concord chambers were amply sized at the start, and enlarged in 1864. At 400 members, New Hampshire's legislature in the forth-largest deliberative body in the English-speaking world (after only the British House of Commons, the U.S. House of Representatives, and India's House of the People). It has always been a matter of pride in the Granite State for each legislator to represent as few constituents as possible. The first state House of Representatives, assembled in 1783, had 87 members, or one for each 100 families in the state. Things are only 10 times less cozy today. With membership at the allowable state maximum of 400 (375 is the minimum), each house member answers to about 2,300 individuals. (Just to make things appropriately bicameral, there's also a 24-member Senate.) Each member of the state legislature receives $100 a year in pay, exclusive of mileage allotments; at $42,400, New Hampshire's entire budget for 424 legislators' pay is a good deal less that the state of New York shells out to each of its assembly-men—and they aren't even required to be on a first-name basis with every last soul they represent.

On the outside chance that you are not a member of the New Hampshire State legislature, there is a visitors' center on the first floor of the State House, to the right of the entrance. Aside from the legislative chambers, the principal interior attractions of the clean-lined, neoclassical structure are the Hall of Flags, containing the ensigns carried by New Hampshire units in all the nation's wars (the First New Hampshire was said to be the first regiment to go to the front, fully uniformed and equipped, when Abraham Lincoln put out a call for volunteers in 1861); and a portrait gallery containing paintings of the state's political, military and civic notables. Alongside the picture of astronaut-suited Alan Shepard is a display featuring moon rocks and a state flag carried on Shepard's lunar mission.

New Hampshire's most famous sons have been immortalized in three dimensions, as bronze statues on the State House Plaza. These include Revolutionary General John Stark, hero of the Battle of Bennington; Franklin Pierce, the Granite State's only president; anti-slavery champion John Parker Hale; and "the godlike Daniel"—Daniel Webster, born in Salisbury and trained at Exeter and Dartmouth.

Cross Park Street from the State House Plaza to visit three of Concord's most popular points of interest. The first, immediately to the left of St. Paul's Episcopal Church, is the Upham-Walker House. Built in 1831 in a late country Federal style bordering on Greek Revival, the house first belonged to Nathaniel Upham, a future New Hampshire Superior Court justice and political ally of Franklin Pierce. The house remained in private hands for nearly a century and a half, surviving throughout that time in its original condition. The state acquired the property in 1979, but not most of the contents. Having appropriated $20,000 for the purpose of buying the house's furnishings at auction, the government watched as they brought more than $300,000. Half of the state appropriation went for two oriental

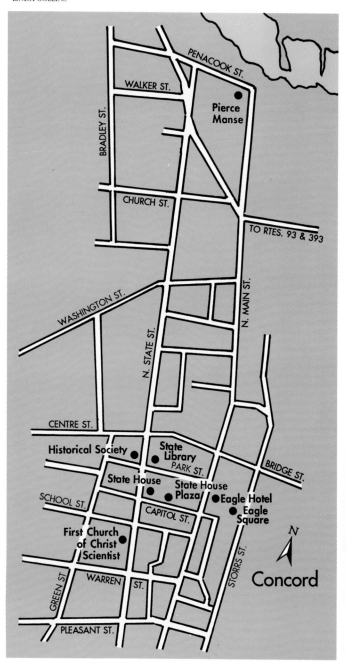

New Hampshire's is the nation's oldest state capitol in which a legislature still meets in its original chambers.

Facing page: The birthplace of Daniel Webster, Franklin. When the boy Daniel was born, his father Ebenezer Webster was serving in the Continental Army. His farm was part of the town of Salisbury in those days.

Above: *The New Hampshire Historical Society, Concord. The sculpture over the entrance is by Daniel Chester French.* ***Facing page:*** *On the capitol lawn, a replica of the Liberty Bell that matches the dimension and tone of the original. It was one of 53 cast in France in 1950 to kick off the U.S. Savings Bond Independence Drive.*

carpets. Still, the house has been suitably furnished, and now is open to visitors.

Directly to the left of the Upham-Walker House is the New Hampshire State Library, oldest such state institution in the United States. The present structure, dedicated in 1895, was built to house the state Supreme Court as well as the library (the Court moved to separate quarters in 1970). Constructed of red Conway granite with gray Concord granite trim in an Italian Renaissance style, the library looks much the same on the outside as it did when it was opened, but has been so heavily remodeled inside that it now incorporates six levels behind its two-story facade. The most recent renovation was in 1972, when, in a fit of modernizing fury, the marble mosaic floor of the main hall was covered with wall-to-wall carpeting.

Next on the left, across North State Street, is the headquarters and museum of the New Hampshire Historical Society. Designed by Guy Lowell, who was also the architect of the Museum of Fine Arts in Boston, the Historical Society's 1911 building is another essay in Concord's favorite construction material, granite. (In this case, the stone was quarried right in town, at Rattlesnake Hill.) What immediately catches the eye in this orderly neoclassical structure, however, is not the stone it is made of, but the stone that was carved and placed over the entrance. The symbolic group is the work of Daniel Chester French, an Exeter native whose best-known sculpture is the seated Abraham Lincoln at the Lincoln Memorial in Washington, D.C. The Concord figures are appropriate to the portals of a historical society: the female figure represents the spirit of the study of ancient history, while the male symbolizes modern history and the contemporary spirit of discovery. Fortunately, the spirit of wanton renovation is given short shrift. When you walk beneath French's sculptures into the Historical Society's rotunda, you can enjoy the same French marble floors and Sienese gray marble walls and ceiling that were installed at the time of construction in 1911. The pursestrings behind all this extravagance were not those of a state comptroller, but of the financier Edward Tuck, who donated the funds for construction. Tuck, a New Hampshireman who spent a good part of his 96 years building a fortune in France, was also the donor of the Dartmouth school of administration and finance named after his father, Amos Tuck. Tuck's contribution to the Historical Society included the Revolutionary War-era American flags that hang over the main staircase. These were captured from a New Hampshire regiment by General Burgoyne's troops during the Battle of Fort Ticonderoga in 1777, and taken back to England. Tuck acquired them in 1913 and donated them to the Historical Society.

A good part of the Society's public area is given to temporary exhibits on New Hampshire history and culture, although there are several permanent exhibits that are key to an appreciation of Concord's own past. The most important of these is the colorful stagecoach right inside the main entrance.

Conveyances of this type were known generically throughout the 19th century as "Concord Coaches." They were manufactured by the Abbot-Downing Company, founded in Concord in 1813 as a wagon-building concern and destined to become the General Motors of the era of horse-powered travel. Abbot-Downing's Concord shops, which covered several acres and employed more than 200 workers, made coaches used throughout the world—notably in the Western stage services operated by firms such as Wells-Fargo, and since etched into American folklore by Stagecoach and countless other Hollywood films. The coach on display here never careened through volleys of Indian arrows on the Great Plains, but was instead assigned to the more prosaic but infinitely safer run between Lanesborough and Gloucester, Massachusetts. In this type of service, the 900-pound carriage would have been drawn by four to six horses, and carried as many as nine inside passengers. Sturdily built of elm and white oak with poplar body panels and wheels of ash and hickory, a coach like this one cost about $1200 during the 1870s, including paint and decorations. For that price, purchasers received an up-to-date bit of Abbot-Downing tech-

PIERCE HOMESTEAD

The Pierce Homestead was built in 1804 by Benjamin Pierce, a general in the American Revolution, twice governor of New Hampshire (1827~28, 1829~30), and father of Franklin Pierce, the 14th President of the United States (1853~57). Franklin Pierce was born in Hillsboro November 23, 1804 and the family occupied this dwelling shortly thereafter.

nology: suspension and shock-absorption was provided by leather "thoroughbrackes," straps slung beneath the body and connecting it to the frame. And all parts were standardized. The idea of uniform replacements did not begin with Henry Ford.

If you backtrack from the Historical Society across the State House grounds and follow North State Street south to School Street, you'll reach a church—granite, of course—built not by the local representatives of a faith headquartered in London or Rome, but by a lady from the neighboring town of Bow. If you walked through the main-floor galleries of the State House, you probably saw her portrait— Mary Baker Eddy, founder of the Christian Science Association. The first Christian Science service in Concord took place on the site of this church in 1897, just 21 years after the association was founded in Boston; four years later, in 1901, Mrs. Eddy dedicated the present structure.

The Concord First Church of Christ Scientist contains an exhibit of photographs chronicling the life of Mary Baker Eddy, and can be toured by arrangement with the Christian Science Reading Room at 34 North Main Street.

At the north end of Concord center, on Penacook Street near North Main, stands the Concord home of the 14th president of the United States, Franklin Pierce. Pierce was born in a log cabin in Hillsborough in 1804, the son of a man who would later be governor of New Hampshire. By the time he was 27, the younger Pierce was speaker of the state House of Representatives; during the Mexican War, he served as a brigadier general under the man who would later oppose him for the presidency, General Winfield Scott. Following a five-year term in the U.S. Senate, Franklin Pierce moved into this 1838 Greek Revival house. During this time he practiced law and circulated his opinions through a column in the Concord Monitor-Patriot, which he owned. His presidency (1853-1857) is generally regarded as having been unsuccessful, largely because by maintaining his Democrat states-rights position he failed to address the problems that were driving a wedge be-

tween North and South in the years before the Civil War. Of course, this leaves open the question of whether an adamant pro-federal stance would merely have hastened open hostility at a time when there was yet no Lincoln to see it through.

Anyway, this is where Franklin Pierce lived— the house, not the location; the building was moved to Penacook Street from its original Concord site in 1971. Many of the furnishings and paintings in the Pierce Manse, as it is called, were nonetheless Pierce family property. The house and its contents offer a detailed look at the life of a middle-class family in mid–19th-century America, during a period when that family just happened to be on its way to the White House.

LAUNA ERNE

Above: *Arguably the greatest legal intellect America has produced, and the greatest American New Hampshire has produced: Daniel Webster.*
Facing page: *The Pierce Homestead at Concord, built in 1804 by President Franklin Pierce's father, New Hampshire Governor Benjamin Pierce.*

5 Dartmouth/Hanover
Vox Clamantis in Deserto

44

I t is a small college," Daniel Webster once said in defense of Dartmouth, his alma mater, "but yet there are those who love it." Indeed there are—many more so now than in 1818, when Webster spoke. But beloved though Dartmouth still may be, it is "small" only by the standards of the giant institutions with which it makes up the Ivy League. For a smaller New England town like Hanover, Dartmouth is big enough, and old enough, long since to have obscured any distinction between the campus and the community. To outsiders, Dartmouth is Hanover, and Hanover Dartmouth. This chapter is a walk centered upon the Green, the center of both.

The town does predate the school, although not by very many years. In 1761 Governor Benning Wentworth, that profligate creator of colonial New Hampshire towns (generally to his own benefit, as he was in the habit of keeping the choicest acreage for himself) issued a charter for a tract of 22,400 acres on the east bank of the Connecticut River where Hanover now stands. The parcel was a township in name only for nearly four years, until in the spring of 1765 Colonel Edmund Freeman and his family traveled upriver to carve a farm out of what still was wilderness, marked only by lines on a map in faraway Portsmouth. It was Freeman, by most accounts, who gave the town the name of the ruling English House of Hanover.

Meanwhile, far to the south in Lebanon, Connecticut, Reverend Eleazar Wheelock was contemplating a move of his own, one that would forever change the fledgling village of Hanover. Wheelock ran a Christian school for young Indians, and had been busy raising funds with which to relocate and expand his mission. He sent one of his former pupils, a Mohegan preacher named Samson Occom, on a speaking tour of England to solicit contributions for this venture. Occom must have been an impressive character—quite apart from the proof he offered of the efficacy of the King James Bible and a Latin grammar when applied to a New England native—

because he came back with a pledged endowment of 11,000 pounds sterling and the patronage of the Earl of Dartmouth. Thus fortified, Rev. Wheelock began to entertain invitations from a number of communities that wanted the new school within their borders. Hanover won, through successful use of the same tactic a modern town might use to lure a corporate headquarters to its new office park: it offered land (3,000 acres), money, lumber, and the manpower of its citizens. What the yeomen hoped for in return were prestige and improved real estate values. Little did they suspect they were in for a medical school, a ski jump, computers in every dorm room, the Hanover Inn, more than two dozen fraternity houses, a winter carnival, and one of the great libraries of North America.

King George III granted Rev. Wheelock the charter for Dartmouth in 1769, and the following year saw the minister arrive in Hanover with his books. The later-adopted motto of Dartmouth College—*Vox Clamantis in Deserto*, "A Voice Crying in the Wilderness"—is a quite accurate suggestion of what those earliest years must have been like, with Rev. Wheelock holding classes in a log cabin built on freshly cleared land. Wilderness though it may have been, however, the picture never included many Indians. They simply never showed up. Before long Dartmouth was a white man's college. It graduated four students at its first commencement exercises in 1771 (Governor John Wentworth, Benning's nephew and successor, arrived via a 75-mile road he had built for the occasion from his summer residence in Wolfeborough), and by 1791, when the first Dartmouth Hall was built on the site of the present structure of that name, 49 baccalaureates were awarded. From then on, the college and the town grew in step with each other.

Dartmouth today is, at its core, the liberal arts college it has always aspired to be, but it is a protean institution nonetheless. Aside from boasting one of

Facing page: *Classroom buildings of Dartmouth College, Dartmouth Hall in center, seen from across the college green, looking over the Senior Fence.*

Top: *Augustus Saint-Gaudens' "Little Studio," on his Cornish estate. Note the clerestory windows, built to provide the sculptor with natural light.*
Above: *The gardens at the Saint-Gaudens National Historic Site, Cornish.*
Right: *Saint-Gaudens' Standing Lincoln, on display at his Cornish studio. According to an old anecdote, the sculptor was directed to New Hampshire when he was looking for models for the Lincoln statue. Whatever the reason for his first visit, he fell in love with the state and spent much of his later life here.*

TOP: MARIANNE AUSTIN-McDERMON; ABOVE LEFT: ROBERT PERRON; RIGHT: GEORGE WUERTHNER

the finest mathematics departments in the country, with computer science especially strong, Dartmouth—although still technically a college, and not a university—counts among its graduate facilities the respected Amos Tuck School of Administration and Finance and the Medical School, which is affiliated with two hospitals and a string of community clinics.

Another aspect of Dartmouth, odd perhaps when contrasted with the general reputation of its students as hardworking scholars, is its vaunted standing as a "party school." In its 1985-86 *Insider's Guide to the Colleges,* the Yale *Daily News* even asserted that the campus was the model for the film *Animal House.* Regardless of whether this is true or merely a barb flung from New Haven, the fact is that nearly two thirds of Dartmouth men belong to fraternities, most of which occupy houses in a row along Webster Avenue. (Dartmouth sororities claim about a third of the school's women students.)

If the presence of the fraternities and their enthusiastic approach to weekend steam-letting is suggestive of campus life in the 1950s, another aspect of Dartmouth in the late '80s is more reminiscent of the 1960s. Unlike many other colleges in what commonly has been regarded as a nonpolitical era in student life, Dartmouth has seen a sharp polarization of liberal and conservative opinion on such issues as South African apartheid and academic free speech. A great deal of controversy has surrounded the existence of a student-run, privately funded off-campus newspaper called the *Dartmouth Review,* which consistently takes a stridently right-wing stand on the affairs of the college and the world at large.

Not that we should countenance putting our heads in the sand, but those of us coming to Dartmouth for a day trip instead of an education can manage to avoid taking sides on the subjects of partying or polemicizing too aggressively. Our decision on an approach to Dartmouth, in this case, simply can be a matter of choosing between Interstates 89 and 91, or the smaller river roads that enter Hanover from the north and south. If time permits, one of the latter is clearly the better choice.

If you are heading toward Hanover from the south, get off Vermont's Interstate 91 no farther north than Exit 8 and immediately cross the Connecticut to connect with New Hampshire Route 12A near Claremont. Roughly 10 miles north along 12A is New England's longest covered bridge, a 468-foot wooden span connecting Cornish, New Hampshire with Windsor, Vermont. It was built in 1866, to replace a 1796 bridge destroyed by flood. A ten-cent toll was collected on the Cornish bridge as recently as the 1940s; one wishes that the proceeds had been put aside for perpetual maintenance, as the bridge was allowed to deteriorate until it was necessary to close the crossing in 1986. As of this writing, the target date for reopening the bridge is December 1989.

Two and a half miles past the Windsor bridge is the road leading to the Augustus Saint-Gaudens National Historic Site, open to the public from late May through the end of October. Saint-Gaudens, sculptor of the *Standing Lincoln*, the *Diana* that stood atop New York's old Madison Square Garden, the *Puritan* and the renowned bronze memorials to Robert Gould Shaw (Boston) and Mrs. Henry Adams (Washington), spent summers in Cornish and lived here year-round from 1900 until his death at age 59 in 1907. The story has it that he first was steered toward New Hampshire while researching his *Standing Lincoln*. A New York friend of Saint-Gaudens simply told the sculptor that he would find "plenty of Lincoln-shaped men" in the Granite State to use as models. Whether or not he found any appropriate Lincolns, he did find beautiful sunsets over Vermont's Mt. Ascutney and an old brick tavern on a hilltop in Cornish to watch them from. He named his estate "Aspet" after his father's native village in France, and remodeled it into the imposing mansion now preserved, along with his gardens and studios, on the grounds of the national historic site.

Augustus Saint-Gaudens was in the vanguard of a movement that made Cornish an artists' and writers' colony of considerable repute during the years between 1885 and 1935. Among the leading lights of the "Cornish Colony" were the novelist

King George III chartered Dartmouth College in 1769; four students graduated in its first commencement two years later.

47

ROBERT PERRON

LAUNA ERNE

Above: *At 468 feet, this span between Windsor, Vermont and Cornish, New Hampshire is the longest covered bridge in New England. Built in 1866, it recently has undergone extensive repairs that will allow it to once again carry automobile traffic.*
Right: *The Lyme Inn, in the Connecticut Valley town of Lyme, is every bit the quintessential New England country inn. The building dates to 1809.*
Facing page: *Robinson Hall, headquarters of Dartmouth student activities including the venerable Dartmouth Outing Club.*

Winston Churchill and the painter-illustrator Maxfield Parrish. Parrish built a home and studio in Plainfield, just north of Cornish, in 1898 when he was 28. He died there 68 years later, just as the popularity of his luminously vivid, fantasy-inspired poster art was coming back into vogue.

From Plainfield, it is roughly 13 miles to Hanover and the Dartmouth campus.

The best northern approach to Hanover is via State Route 10, which winds south from Woodsville along the east bank of the Connecticut. Some 10 miles north of Hanover, Route 10 passes through the town of Lyme, which was chartered in 1761 and was once the sheep-raising capital of New England. Lyme is the home of the Dartmouth Skiway, a downhill facility open to the public. But the most outstanding attraction here is the village itself, clustered around a big, grassy town common and towered over by a white Congregational Church built in 1812. The big frame house across the street from the church is three years older, and today is the Lyme Inn. The inn answers to its archetypal role, no less than the common and the church: if you have a mental image of a quintessential New England hostelry complete with antiques, fireplaces, four-poster beds and a homey tavern, the Lyme Inn likely will fit it splendidly, and feed you well to boot. It is one of the preferred lodging places to use during a trip to Dartmouth, the other being the much larger, more hotel-like Hanover Inn located directly on the College Green in Hanover.

A tour of the Dartmouth campus itself might best begin right on the Green, and in fact need not stray far from this broad lawn as most of the buildings of architectural or historic interest to outsiders border it almost directly. (If you are a prospective student, more-detailed tours begin at the Admissions Office in McNutt Hall on North Main Street; other escorted tours must be arranged through the college's Public Relations office.)

One curious feature of the Green, hardly likely to be noticed at all by casual passers-by, is the "senior fence" occupying a short stretch of the walkway along North Main Street. The fence is a simple affair of green wooden rails and granite posts, donated by the Class of 1897 and expanded by the Class of 1923. According to guidebooks of a half century ago, the fence was covered with carved initials, put there by generations of college seniors —the only class allowed to sit on the rails. The fence's modern aspect suggests an interesting contrast between two styles of collegiate life. I've never seen anyone sitting on it, seniors or otherwise, and today's wooden rails bear nary an initial. The conclusions are obvious: college students don't sit around anymore; and initial-carving has gone entirely out of vogue. Perhaps there are pipe-smoking shades in ectoplasmic letter sweaters slouched around the senior fence, wondering why everyone is so busy.

Two of the buildings opposite the senior fence on North Main Street are Robinson and McNutt halls. Robinson is noteworthy as the main campus headquarters of the Dartmouth Outing Club, as strong an extracurricular outdoor sports organization as can be found in any college in the United States. The Club's raison d'etre is to make full use of Dartmouth's incomparable location between the Green and the White mountains, and its programs include hiking, climbing, cross-country and downhill skiing, and canoeing. Another Outing Club activity unheard-of on the vast majority of American campuses is ski jumping. Dartmouth's 45-meter jump is located at the Hanover Country Club, on the northern outskirts of town one mile from the Green via Route 10. More than 20 American Olympic jumpers have trained here, including the 1988 U.S. team's Mike Holland, who once set a world record with a jump of 186 meters (the Hanover jump's record is $51\frac{1}{2}$ meters). Spectators can watch the Dartmouth Outing Club's recreational jumpers as well as ski school, high school and college team members practice on Monday, Wednesday and Friday evenings during the winter. For serious competition, there's the Roger Burt Memorial Jump, held each January, and the February jump held as part of Dartmouth's time-honored Winter Carnival.

LAUNA ERNE

Above: *Administration buildings, Dartmouth College.*
Right: *It's difficult to authenticate a claim such as "world's largest snowman," which was made for this Dartmouth Winter Carnival behemoth in 1987. But we are certain that this was the largest snowman ever to have played the saxophone.*
Facing page: *A panel of the richly allegorical murals by Mexican artist Jose Clemente Orozco, painted 1932-1934 in the lower level of the Baker Library at Dartmouth College. Titled "Modern Migration of the Spirit," this panel juxtaposes a militant, resurrected Christ figure against the modern machinery of war and the detritus of eastern and western systems of belief.*

TED LEVIN

The Winter Carnival, a Dartmouth tradition since 1911, is an extravagantly staged throwback to the days when seniors carved their initials in fences. A week-long celebration built around parties, dances and a profusion of winter sports competitions, its most visible manifestation for outsiders is the fanciful display of enormous snow sculptures on the Green. Some of these creations take three or four days of work on the part of crews fielded by fraternities and other student organizations; the works are hopelessly ephemeral, and the pace of their transformation to slush is entirely at the whim of Hanover's late-winter climate. During the process, they are likely to re-semble some strange imagining of Claes Oldenberg or Salvador Dali.

Dartmouth's Winter Carnival, incidentally, was the inspiration for the 1939 Hollywood film *Winter Carnival*, starring Ann Sheridan as a divorcee in love with a professor. The novelist Budd Schulberg (*What Makes Sammy Run?*), who was serving his time as a screenwriter in those days, was a co-author of the script. A 1936 graduate of Dartmouth, he presumably knew whereof he spoke. *Winter Carnival* is in late-night purgatory now, but the original is still fresh as new snow.

Just a year after the 1939 premiere of "Winter Carnival," history was made in a somewhat more serious vein in McNutt Hall when a computer in a distant city was programmed via a telephone link originating here. This was the first time computer instructions were transmitted from a remote location. This was one of the first in a long line of Dartmouth computer accomplishments, which include the development of the BASIC language by John Kemeny, a former president of the college.

Turn right from North Main onto Wentworth Street, then left in the middle of the block, and you will be facing the serene Georgian facade of the Baker Memorial Library. Baker, the central library of the Dartmouth campus, was the 1928 gift of New York banker George Fisher Baker, who dedicated it to the memory of his uncle Fisher Ames Baker, Dartmouth 1859. Although most of the building is necessarily taken up by stacks and reading rooms, two areas are of particular interest to visitors. The Hough Room (left after you enter the library, then right at the end of the hall) is a sumptuous chamber resembling a 19th-century gentleman's study, its walls lined with the rarest and most valuable books in the Dartmouth College collections. Here are more than 150 volumes of incunabula (books printed before 1501; the word is Latin for "in the cradle" and refers to the infancy of printing with moveable type); the Hickmott Shakespeare Collection, including copies of all four folios, nearly 40 quarto volumes, all known pre-1700 editions of *Macbeth*, and much of the playwright's source material; and more than 200 volumes representing the finest achievements of the bookbinder's art. American material includes all first and limited editions of Stephen Crane; a comprehensive Melville collection including important volumes of criticism as well as an exhaustive survey of more than 130 years of editions of *Moby-Dick*; and—in a display case at the center of the room—the first three volumes of the enormous "elephant folio" edition of John James Audubon's *Birds of America* in the original copies owned by Daniel Webster. The speculation is that Webster didn't own Volume Four because he didn't pay Audubon for the first three.

One flight below the Baker Library's entrance hall, the walls of a basement reading room are painted with as remarkable a series of murals as exist in New England. They were painted by Jose Clemente Orozco between 1932 and 1934, during which time the Mexican artist taught in Dartmouth's art department. Executed in an angular, stylized realism, with an expressive use of color, the murals depict the progress (or anti-progress, depending on how one sees it) of civilization in the Americas, from the rise of the Aztecs through the triumph of the European interlopers to the modern ascendancy of an exploitative, technocratic society and the prospects for redemption. The central figure of Orozco's mythos is the Aztec deity Quetzalcoatl, and each of the fourteen major panels that make up the work is heavily laden with symbols—sometimes obvious, often ob-

Above: *Dartmouth's Webster Hall, with the belfry of Baker Library in the background.*
Facing page: *The clear light of reason: Dartmouth's Baker Library.*

scure. An explanatory pamphlet, available at the library, is recommended for anyone who wishes to take more than a cursory look at the Orozco murals.

Continuing in a clockwise direction around the College Green, the building immediately past Baker Library (on the corner of Wentworth and College Streets) is Webster Hall, a 1907 brick neo-classical auditorium named in honor of the man Dartmouth has always considered its greatest alumnus. Daniel Webster, Dartmouth 1801, was a New Hampshire native who in 1818 had just finished serving two terms as a congressman from the Granite State. Already in possession of a considerable legal reputation, he was called upon that year by his alma mater to serve as a counsel in a Supreme Court case that could have ended in the college's disestablishment.

The trouble had started in 1816, when the New Hampshire legislature passed a bill that superseded the original college charter and created a "Dartmouth University" with overseers appointed by the governor. As president, the state installed Eleazer Wheelock's son John, who had been president of the college for 36 years before a falling-out with the trustees led to his removal in 1815.

The heavy-handed state action did not sit well with Dartmouth College trustees, faculty and students, most of whom ignored the existence of the "university" and held their own classes. The intolerable parallel existence of two Dartmouths was clearly a matter for the courts to resolve. The college trustees sued to establish the inviolability of their 1769 contract, and the case eventually was heard by the U.S. Supreme Court under Chief Justice John Marshall. It was during his final argument that Daniel Webster uttered his famous "it is a small college, but there are those who love it." The court found for the trustees, "Dartmouth University" disappeared from the books, and an important precedent was set concerning federal protection of existing charters and contracts.

Directly across College Street from Webster Hall is Rollins Chapel, oddly enough for the Granite State the only building on campus constructed on the state's signature stone. Built in 1855, it clearly presages the Richardsonian Romanesque architecture of the latter decades of the 19th century, with its use of broad arches and the heavy massing of its constituent parts.

As you head up College Street, the next row of structures facing the Green comprise "Dartmouth Row," the best known, most photographed cluster of buildings on campus. Stark white against the lawns and trees, Wentworth, Dartmouth, Thornton and Reed halls are as beautifully unified an example of collegiate architecture as can be found in America. In their Georgian simplicity, they hark back to the vernacular of the New England churches and meetinghouses of Dartmouth's earliest years.

Wentworth and Thornton Halls, built along axes perpendicular to the street, serve as virtual bookends for the serene, 150-foot facade of Dartmouth Hall. This three-story cupola-topped building is a 1904 brick replica of the original Dartmouth Hall, a wooden structure built on this site in 1791, which for many years housed virtually the entire college. Until 1845, in fact, Dartmouth Row comprised the entire campus. When the original Dartmouth Hall burned in 1904, alumni poured in contributions to immediately replace a building that by then had almost talismanic significance.

College Street ends at Wheelock Street. Here is the entrance to the Hopkins Center, a concert auditorium, and the Hood Museum, housing Dartmouth's fine arts collections. Immediately to the right of the Hopkins Center is the Hanover Inn, a posh, privately-run hostelry that answers the need for a "dorm" for visiting alumni and parents.

Turn from East Wheelock onto South Main Street, on the corner by the Hanover Inn, to leave the college proper and enter the college town. South Main is abustle with shops, taverns and restaurants; you can stop in at Bentley's for a Catamount Ale, made in a tiny brewery just across the river in Vermont, and browse through the hundreds of marked-down volumes on the sidewalk tables in front of the Dartmouth Bookstore. Buy a Dartmouth sweatshirt, and say you've been to the Ivy League.

6 Around Lake Winnipesaukee

It was built at Alton Bay on Lake Winnipesaukee, and launched in the spring of 1872. The builders, the Boston and Maine Railroad, named it *Mt. Washington* and spent the then-princely sum of $62,000 to assure its status as the most powerful and most elegant steamboat on the lake. *Mt. Washington* was 178 feet long from stem to stern, with a beam of nearly 50 feet and a 450-horsepower engine. With elegant salons and elaborately laid table—at least in the days before Prohibition telescoped the length and enjoyment of cruise ship meals—it inspired passengers with a loyalty as unshakeable as that of White Mountains resort patrons for their favorite grand hotels. The *Mt. Washington* turned its side paddles through the waters of Lake Winnipesaukee for 67 seasons, until a dockside fire leaped to its old timbers in December of 1939 and burnt the boat to the waterline. At the time, it was the oldest steamboat in regular service on the inland waters of the United States.

The long career of the *Mt. Washington*, and the special place the boat occupied in the hearts of New Hampshire people and out-of-staters alike, serves to underline an important fact about the Granite State: this is as much a place of lakes as of mountains. The biggest of those lakes, in terms of sheer size, of lore and of popularity, is Lake Winnipesaukee.

Winnipesaukee, whose shores sprawl irregularly along a northwest-to-southeast axis near the center of New Hampshire, takes its name from an Indian word roughly translated as "smile of the Great Spirit." The story goes that centuries ago Ellacoya, daughter of Chief Ahanton of the Penacooks who lived along the northern shores of the lake, was courted by Kona, the chief of a hostile tribe to the south. Ahanton was at first enraged to find Ellacoya in love with his sworn enemy, but Ellacoya prevailed on her father not to kill Kona. Impressed as much by Kona's bravery as with his daughter's Pocahontas-style entreaties, Ahanton gave the couple his blessing. After the wedding feast, Kona and Ellacoya set out under stormy skies for Kona's village—but at the moment their canoe reached the middle of the lake, ready to head off on its own from the rest of the paddling tribe, the clouds parted and the sun emerged to sparkle on the waters.

People like stories about doe-eyed Indian maidens melting their fathers' hard hearts, and this explanation of the naming of New Hampshire's big lake survives in spite of the plausibility of the Great Spirit's smiling on the waters of Winnipesaukee for no better reason than a sunrise or sunset. In any event, the tale accounts for the name of the scenic state park and beach on the lake between West Alton and Glendale: Ellacoya.

Legends and apocrypha aside, archaeological evidence suggests a long Indian association with the Lake Winnipesaukee area. The Penacook encampment Aquadochtan, along the once-narrow stream that connects Paugus Bay to the lake proper, is believed to have been one of the largest seasonal Indian communities in New England. Discoveries of quantities of arrowheads, stone knives, household artifacts and even gravesites verify the importance of this site. The reason for its prominence was fishing. For generations, the Indians maintained a stone fish trap, or weir, that reached across the mouth of the Paugus Bay passage; fragments of it remained, near the city of Laconia's Endicott Rock public beach at the present Weirs Beach, until the passage was deepened and widened earlier in this century to accommodate larger pleasure boats.

The town in whose name the old Indian weir survives is easily the gaudiest, and in summer the busiest, of Lake Winnipesaukee's shoreside communities. Weirs Beach is a little bit of Asbury Park, New Jersey in New Hampshire, with video arcades, bowling alleys (the small local variety, using the diminutive "candlepins"), water slides and wave pools, miniature golf, and even an annual Miss Winnipesaukee pageant. It's also the midway station for the Win-

Facing page: *Once a steam-driven side-wheeler on Lake Champlain, the* Mount Washington *now is a twin-engine diesel vessel on Lake Winnipesaukee, here near Moultonborough.*

nipesaukee Railroad, which runs diesel-powered excursion trains between Lakeport and Meredith. Best of all, Weirs Beach is the home port of the original S.S. *Mt. Washington*'s successor, the M.V. *Mount Washington* (S.S. for steamship, M.V. for motor vessel).

No sooner had the old *Mt. Washington* burned than the owner, Captain Leander Lavallee, started making plans to replace it. Capt. Lavallee, who had bought the *Mt. Washington* from the Boston and Maine in 1922, had two options: he could buy a new boat, which at that time would have cost upwards of $250,000 (he had reportedly paid the B&M $3,000 for the 50-year-old *Mt. Washington*), or he could shop for a used vessel. Choosing the latter course, Capt. Lavallee purchased the 203' iron-hull steamboat *Chateaugay*, an 1888 Lake Champlain passenger packet that had been converted to an automobile ferry in 1925. The price was $20,000.

In order to transport *Chateaugay* from Burlington, Vermont to Lake Winnipesaukee, Capt. Lavalee had the superstructure removed and the hull cut into 20 sections for rail shipment to Lakeport, on Paugus Bay south of Weirs Beach. Once reassembled, the hull was fitted with a new superstructure and two triple-expansion steam engines driving propellors rather than side wheels. Rechristened *Mt. Washington II*, the boat was launched on Winnipesaukee in August 1940.

There was to be yet another round of modifications. *Mt. Washington II* never ran satisfactorily with the new steam engines, and wartime shortages cut into her own fuel supplies as well as those of the travelers who had come in years past to cruise Lake Winnipesaukee. Capt. Lavallee's company went bankrupt and, after the war, new owners refitted the old steamship with twin diesel engines. With a few modifications in her superstructure, she re-emerged as the M.V. *Mount Washington*. This is the vessel that sails out of Weirs Beach today, taking passengers on $3\frac{1}{4}$-hour, 50-mile cruises on a regular schedule between late May and late October (there are also special dinner cruises, complete with live music).

Even if you don't get a chance to take passage on the *Mount Washington*, it's worth timing a visit to Weirs Beach to see the boat head majestically in and out of port.

The *Mount Washington* isn't the only large motor vessel to offer public excursions on Lake Winnipesaukee. The *Doris E* and the *Sophie C* make regular summer rounds, also beginning and ending at Weirs Beach. *Sophie C* is a mail boat, latest in a line of steam and motor craft that have delivered the U.S. Mail to the lake's island dwellers. There are 274 habitable islands in Lake Winnipesaukee—some quite large, like 750-acre Bear Island, the Appalachian Mountain Club's Three Mile Island (named for its distance from Center Harbor, and not after the infamous nuclear power plant), and some small, privately-owned outcrops barely large enough to support a summer cottage and a boat house. A number of Winnipesaukee's islands have come under the protection of the Lakes Region Conservation Trust, a non-profit organization that protects environmentally sensitive lands either through securing conservation easements or by outright ownership. Among the Trust's properties are the bulk of Stonedam Island, the lake's largest undeveloped island; and Ragged and Little Ragged Islands. The Ragged Island Nature Center is the site of a summer conservation education program, as is the Stonedam Island Wildlife Preserve.

The next town north of Weirs Beach, on Route 3 along the right side of Lake Winnipesaukee, is Meredith—the self-proclaimed "latchkey to the White Mountains." Before Interstate 93 was built through the Pemigewasset Valley west of here, the latchkey metaphor meant a good deal more; but in any event, Meredith is still a good staging ground for further exploration of the shores of Winnipesaukee and smaller nearby lakes. If you head north on U.S. 3 (also state route 25 west along this stretch), you'll pass through East Holderness and Holderness on the south shore of Squam Lake, famous as the locale of the film *On Golden Pond*. Squam has an entirely different personality than Winnipesaukee; instead of

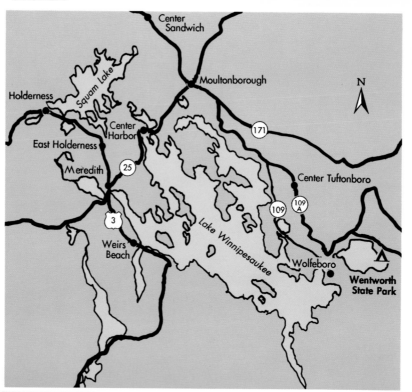

Lake Winnipesaukee's 274 habitable islands range from 750-acre Bear Island to small, privately-owned outcrops that support only a summer cottage and a boat house apiece.

Left: *The stuff of which jack-o-lanterns are made, heaped before a fine center-entrance colonial house in Meredith.* **Facing page:** *Running before a stiff breeze, Lake Winnipesaukee.*

Weirs Beach-style entertainment, condo developments and heavy summer pleasure-boat traffic, here you'll find quiet summer cottages set unobtrusively back from the shore. More likely, you won't find them at all, since that's precisely the idea.

Bear to the right at Meredith, and you'll follow Route 25 east to the village of Center Harbor. Following this route calls for an almost immediate detour—just outside of Meredith center is the right-hand turnoff onto the narrow road that heads to the end of Meredith Neck. The property along the shore on both sides and at the end of the neck is private, but the five-mile (each way) side trip is worthwhile for its pretty views of rolling meadows and forest.

Center Harbor, once clustered with small summer hotels, is now a quieter community of private homes and a fine old-fashioned hostelry, the Red Hill Inn, with views of Squam Lake and the southern reaches of the White Mountains. The inn occupies a 35-room mansion built in 1904, and very nearly burned down for fire department practice before its 1985 salvation by the present innkeepers. Center Harbor (named not for its location but for two brothers named Senter who had a land grant here) has become something of a cross-country ski mecca; the Longwood Ski Touring Center is right nearby.

Center Harbor offers another of the which-way-should-we-go choices common to the towns and byways of the lakes region, as if in homage to New Hampshireman Robert Frost's two roads diverging. The back road that runs north out of town skirts the eastern shoreline of Squam Lake (it's the only road to do so, for any appreciable distance), and leads to the attractive village of Center Sandwich. Center Sandwich is famous as the place where the League of New Hampshire Craftsmen got its start. The League's predecessor, Sandwich Home Industries, was the 1926 creation of Mrs. J. Randolph Coolidge, a wealthy Massachusetts native who cared deeply about the livelihoods of the farm and village people living near her New Hampshire home. Mrs. Coolidge encouraged the preservation, practice and teaching of traditional home artisanry, and helped set up a

GEORGE WUERTHNER

LAUNA ERNE

Above: *The magic of Fonda, Hepburn and the loons: This inn is taking only slight license with its name, since* On Golden Pond *was filmed here on Squam Lake.*

Left: *Center Sandwich, just north of Winnipesaukee and Squam lakes. This is the birthplace of the organization that grew to become the League of New Hampshire Craftsmen.*

Facing page: *A Lake Winnipesaukee marina. Crowding of boats on New Hampshire's big lake is becoming a serious problem.*

59

shop where the natives could sell their handcrafts. In 1931 the state government got behind the idea, and the League of Arts and Crafts—later the League of New Hampshire Craftsmen—began to establish stores throughout the state. The descendant of the original shop is still here, selling everything from pottery to handcrafted toys to homemade jams and jellies. Center Sandwich, too, has a comfortable place to stay, the 1849 Corner House Inn. There are are only four guest rooms, so reserve well in advance.

If you stay on Route 25 east out of Center Harbor—taking a scenic side-trip down to the end of Moultonborough Neck, a forked peninsula that reaches far into Lake Winnipesaukee—the next town is Moultonborough, where, shortly after the turn of the century, Thomas Gustave Plant built the most extravagant, most grandly situated private home the Lakes Region ever has seen. Plant called his 6,000-acre estate Lucknow, after a Scottish castle, and crowned it with a $7 million stone mansion that commanded views of Lake Winnipesaukee and the White Mountains over a 75-mile radius. Like most of the magnificoes of his day, Plant left no heirs remotely capable of maintaining such an establishment in the cost climate of the late 20th century. So, like Hearst's San Simeon and most of the stately homes of England, Lucknow today belongs to the paying public. "The Castle in the Clouds" is its commercial name, and in addition to offering tours of the house and grounds, the management maintains more than 80 miles of bridle trails and offers horse rentals. It is the view, though, that really makes a visit here worthwhile.

South of Moultonborough, Route 109 drifts down the east shore of Lake Winnipesaukee—stay on 109 proper for lake views and a short ride to the end of Tuftonborough Neck; bear left onto 109A to pass through Tuftonborough Center, where a general store claims to be the oldest in continuous operation in the United States. Both roads lead into Wolfeboro, the largest town on Lake Winnipesaukee (we aren't counting Laconia, which has frontage only on Paugus Bay). Wolfeboro calls itself America's oldest

summer resort, and for an interesting reason. It was here, on the lake later named after him, that colonial governor John Wentworth built his country estate starting in 1769. No one, public official or wealthy private citizen, ever had selected a summer home site so far out in the wilderness at that early date, and the logistics of the manor's construction and supply made it all the more impressive. Governor Wentworth manicured 600 of his 6,000 acres into an English-style park, stocked with deer, and set his main house and outbuildings above a lawn a quarter mile from the lake. The fine interior woodwork and furnishings were brought from Portsmouth by pack horse, then ferried across Winnipesaukee and the governor's own lake by flat-bottomed gundalows. The house was 100 feet long, with two tall stories (the first-floor ceilings were eighteen feet high) and six-foot windows; the keys to the front door weighed a pound and a half each. To reach his summer mansion from the colonial capital at Portsmouth, Wentworth had a 45-mile road built; in 1771, he extended this wilderness thoroughfare another 67 miles to Hanover so he could travel by coach to the first commencement exercises at Dartmouth College.

Governor Wentworth and his wife, Lady Frances, didn't have many years in which to enjoy their back-country Versailles. In 1775, before construction on the estate was finished, they were forced into exile by the onset of the American Revolution; but within a few years, Wentworth secured for himself the governorship of Nova Scotia. At Halifax he built the magnificent Province House, still the official residence of the lieutenant governor, which stands as a monument to the Wentworth idea of how the king's appointed executive ought to live. The mansion on Lake Wentworth is gone, though, burnt to the ground in 1820, the year of Wentworth's death. Only a cellar hole remains, on the grounds of Wentworth State Park.

The era to follow on and around Lake Winnipesaukee would belong to the steamboats, and to the summer hotels frequented by ordinary souls.

NONA BAUER

Above: *The doughty little Doris E is one of Lake Winnipesaukee's smaller summer excursion boats.*
Left: *Melvin Village, a tidy little crossroads on the east shore of Lake Winnepisaukee.*
Facing page: *Yes, the dog is windsurfing. No, he is not wearing a personal flotation device. The setting is Lake Winnipesaukee, near Moultonborough.*

GEORGE WUERTHNER

61

7 In & Out of North Conway

The resort scene in the White Mountains of a hundred years ago was much more a matter of hotels than of towns. Although places like Bethlehem (see Chapter 9) could boast a concentration of seasonal hostelries in a village setting, most vacationers were attracted to the big, self-contained establishments such as the Crawford House, the Mountain View House and Fabyan's. The towns that dotted the valleys of New Hampshire's north county were railroad depots and places where farmers went to market. There might be a few boarding houses for summer people without the means or the inclination to put up at the big hotels, but by and large the notion of small towns as vacation destinations had not yet arrived.

As much as anything else, downhill skiing turned this situation around. When the alpine craze struck the mountains of Vermont and New Hampshire in the 1930s, the typical ski area was established within a short distance of a town large enough to offer accommodations as well as rail connections with major population centers. Even if skiers headed upcountry in their own cars, they needed village lodgings; in the days before the sport of skiing became the "ski industry," there were no such things as town house condominiums or motel units at the feet of the slopes. For a place like North Conway, the coming of skiing and ski people meant that an entirely new phase of development was about to begin—and to change drastically, as the postwar era saw one style of travel replace another. If we can look to North Conway and environs to see how the sociology of skiing has changed over the past 50 years, we can just as surely take this region as clear evidence of what skiing has done for (some might say "to") the White Mountains in general.

North Conway, which is not technically a political entity but one of two major settlements in the town of Conway (Conway itself is the other), has been around a good deal longer than the nearby ski areas, the railroad, or even the road through Pinkham Notch. The first white settler in these parts was a Scotch-Irish veteran of the French and Indian War named Andrew McMillan. McMillan was the recipient of one of colonial Governor Benning Wentworth's generous land grants, which in this instance consisted of a great swath of property along the Saco River's east bank from present-day North Conway to Bartlett. He set himself up here in 1764 as somewhat of a squire, with a huge working farm, a great house and tavern, and a retinue of liveried black servants. The territory was mostly McMillan's own for quite some time, although North Conway eventually become part of the orbit of small farms around the more southerly village of Conway—in its early days a center of light, water-powered industry.

By the middle of the 19th century, the Conway–North Conway area had become an important center for artists associated with the White Mountain School. The most famous of the White Mountain painters was Benjamin Champney, who worked in North Conway about 1850; however, as early as 1830 the Hudson River School pioneer Thomas Cole exhibited his *View Near Conway* at the Royal Academy in London. Later in the century, the landscape master George Inness also painted here. The painters' subject was the surrounding mountains, not the town; nevertheless, it may have been a bit uncharitable for the authors of the Federal Writers Project's 1938 *New Hampshire* to comment that "the village...itself is somewhat unattractive." But the WPA writers can be forgiven. They were making their observations in the days before factory outlets grew along Route 16 in the outskirts of North Conway like mushrooms after a spring rain.

The White Mountain School of artists notwithstanding, the biggest thing ever to hit North Conway was downhill skiing. Before the 1930s, such limited interest as there was in skiing in the United States centered upon a sport that resembled a cross

Facing page: One of New England's most distinctive Victorian buildings, the railroad station at North Conway is today a terminal for seasonal excursion trains.

between the modern Nordic and Alpine techniques. Equipment hadn't yet become specialized; bindings could be loosened at the heel for cross-country travel, and tightened for descending hills. Skiing hadn't yet lent itself to concentrated, highly developed "areas," and about the only means of uphill propulsion other than the herringbone and sidestep maneuvers was the venerable rope tow.

The coming of technically skilled European skiers to New England changed all that, and the new sophistication helped create the demand for manicured slopes graded according to degrees of downhill difficulty. In 1936, North Conway businessman Carroll Reed established an open-enrollment ski school—America's first—at the Eastern Slope Inn, the elegant, white-columned Georgian Revival hotel that still stands at the northern end of the village. As his chief instructor, Reed hired Hannes Schneider, an Austrian émigré who had taught the Tyrolean ski troops in the army of his native country.

Whether they studied under Schneider or not—and regardless of whether or not they belonged to any of the dozens of ski clubs that came into existence throughout New Hampshire in the Thirties—skiers flocked to the North Conway region at first to sample the hell-for-leather delights of Tuckerman Ravine (still a favorite spot for spring skiing, and still without a lift), and later to patronize growing commercial areas such as Mt. Cranmore, Black Mountain, Wildcat and (not until the 1960s) Attitash. There long had been "summer people" in the mountains, and now there was a whole subculture of "winter people" as well.

Although New Hampshire's highway system had advanced sufficiently to allow many skiers to drive to their north-country destinations even in the years before World War II, a good number still preferred to head for the mountains on the Boston & Maine Railroad's famous "snow trains" out of Boston's North Station. Beginning in 1931, these special trains would leave the city for North Conway well before dawn, packed mostly with young people whose weekend spirit took hold as soon as they boarded the cars. Older New Englanders who remember taking the snow trains always recall the singing, laughter, and general sense of bonhomie that characterized the rail trip to North Conway.

Then as now, the dominant architectural feature of North Conway's business district was the brightly painted, fancifully mansarded train station that marked the end of the line for the snow trains and the last stop of any significance for trains heading off to the northwest for the hotels of Crawford Notch. Probably one of the most photographed buildings in New Hampshire even two decades ago when it stood nearly derelict, the North Conway station today is the northern terminus for the Conway Scenic Railway, a seasonal excursion operation featuring antique coaches and parlor cars. There is a small railway museum in the station, and an interesting collection of steam locomotives and passenger stock in the yards out back.

But now that the railroad in these parts has become a tourist attraction rather than a transportation link with the outside world, the town of North Conway has become less of a compact lodging center for skiers and more of a sprawling, strip-mall component of the larger, decentralized service economy that caters to both summer and winter visitors who come and go by automobile. I've seen the change over the past 20 years. As recently as the 1960s, a traveler heading north on Route 16 from Conway—or on Route 302 from Fryeburg, Maine; for a short stretch they're the same road—would pass little more than a few scattered motels and restaurants before the thickly settled center of North Conway, dominated by that lovely confection of a train station, came into view. Nowadays, the distinction between Conway and North Conway has nearly been lost. The frenzy of building along Routes 16/302 that has all but joined the two settlements has not been primarily a matter of catering to dining and lodging needs, but of retailing. Like Freeport, Maine and Manchester, Vermont, North Conway has become a factory outlet capital. On a recent drive toward the town center I took note of three women's designer clothing empo-

LINDA COLLINS

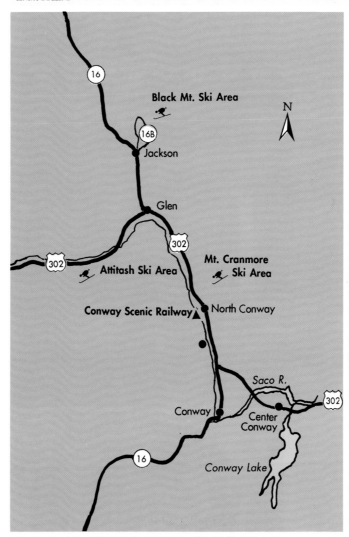

The Conway Scenic Railway today is a tourist attraction rather than a transportation link with the outside world.

Facing page: *The contrast between Jackson (seen here) and North Conway couldn't be more pronounced. There isn't a factory outlet in sight here.*

65

Above: *All aboard! The Conway Scenic Railroad's vintage coaches are ready for a trip along the Saco River Valley.*
Right: *The Conway Scenic Railroad maintains a fleet of steam and diesel motive power for its excursion trips. Several locomotives are always on view in the yards behind the North Conway station.*
Facing page: *The Eastern Slope Inn, North Conway.*

CHERYL McGEE-MILLEY

ria, a men's shirt outlet, an outdoor clothing shop, two shoe stores, and a fashionable sweater establishment…and that was very early in the approach, before I stopped cataloguing for fear that it would distract my attention from the steady stream of bargain hunters entering and leaving the flow of traffic.

Factory outlets are an interesting New England phenomenon. They used to be true to their name, in that they were at or near the places where the things they sold were manufactured—in this part of the country, usually shoes and sport clothing. Most of what they sold were seconds, and the prices were low by anyone's standards. This began to change when manufacturers started noticing that certain small towns and scenic byways drew such a consistent stream of travelers that they just begged to be exploited as prime retail locations. The stores opened in these places were no longer intended simply to serve as outlets for otherwise unsalable merchandise, but to tap an affluent transient market by offering discounts on what are primarily first-quality goods. The people who had gone into business in ski country used to figure that someone up from Boston or New York would spend a certain portion of their waking hours skiing, and the rest eating and drinking. Thus that was the nature of the economy they established. Eventually, though, the brighter lights began to discover that people would just as soon shop as eat, drink or ski—thus the outlet boom. By now, of course, the target market is not just skiers, but year-round visitors to places like North Conway. And having achieved critical mass, the concentration of retail establishments has begun to generate a traffic of its own: there are people who come to North Conway, as they do to Freeport, just to go to the stores. The mountains? They're nice, too.

This is why the principal impression one gets of North Conway these days is of a gigantic traffic jam, and why the WPA guidebook authors of 50 years ago, who sniffed that the town was "somewhat unattractive" would now gladly wish it back to 1938. Resorts have begun to mimic the population centers that they draw from. Just as suburbanization made the old downtown retail areas superfluous, so too has the concept of a "village" of North Conway serving the surrounding ski country become passé. Time was, you'd walk from your lodgings at the Eastern Slope Inn down to Carroll Reed's store, to buy a pair of ski pants. You still can do that today—but you can also drive from your time-sharing condo to the outlet strip and buy a whole season's wardrobe.

Happily, North Conway and environs still can offer more than what the PR people call a "retail experience," and there are a few corners south of Pinkham Notch where you can get out of the fray. I've always been fond of an inn called the Bernerhof, on Route 302 in Glen. It was founded more than 40 years ago by a Swiss violinist named Charlie Zumstein, who had come to the United States to play with his band at the 1939 New York World's Fair and stayed rather than return to a Europe newly engulfed in war. Like a good many émigrés from Germany and Switzerland, Charlie gravitated to the North Conway region, which must have looked as much like home as anyplace in the Northeast. With his gracious wife Claire in charge of the superb Bernerhof kitchen, Charlie played host at his inn in the finest tradition of the continental gentleman. He clicked his heels when he brought you a bottle of wine, not in some arch imitation of the way things used to be done, but because he was one of the people who really used to do things that way. He would appear out of nowhere to light a woman's cigarette, and disappear just as magically. And every year on Swiss Independence Day, he would take his giant alpenhorn down off the wall and bellow out a call to the fat brown cattle ruminating on some flower-strewn mountain slope of his ancestral memory. Charlie Zumstein's portrait—eyes twinkling, violin tucked under his chin—still hangs in an upstairs parlor at his inn, which has gone through several changes of ownership and a considerable enlargement in size since he and Claire passed away in the late 1960s.

The Swiss menu the Zumsteins devised at the Bernerhof remains largely intact. Its foundation is

veal—offered most interestingly as emince de veau, shredded and cooked in white wine—and its national trademark is Emmenthaler and Gruyere cheese, which appear in fondues, in schnitzel cordon bleu, and in the little breaded and sauteed rolls called delices de Gruyere. But only Claire Zumstein, I'm convinced, knew the secret of bringing the proportion of structurally necessary puff paste in this dish down so low that the result seemed to be cylinders of pure melted Gruyere with no visible means of support.

Each fall and spring the Bernerhof serves as campus for A Taste of the Mountains cooking school, run by Boston area chef and food writer Steven Raichlen. Raichlen, an alumnus of the Cordon Bleu in Paris, conducts two- and five-day courses concentrating on classic and modern French styles of cuisine. Students stay at the Bernerhof, and dine on their own cooking as well as the house menu. It all makes for the most rewarding combination of learning and having fun since the snow trains used to deliver pupils to Hannes Schneider's doorstep.

Another pleasant retreat within a few miles' drive of North Conway is Jackson, a tiny village on the other side of a covered bridge to the right of Route 16 between Glen and Pinkham Notch. Jackson is a good place to go if you are feeling politically fickle: first settled in 1778, it took the name of the Federalist Adams on incorporating in 1800, only to change to that of Old Hickory, a Democrat, in 1829. (To paraphrase Jackson, the victors got not only the spoils but their names on the map.) It's also the place for anyone who prefers to walk out the door of his inn after dinner and be met only by the stars and the sound of the river. For lodgings in Jackson I like the Wentworth Hotel, a big, old-fashioned establishment in the shingle style of a century ago, located right on the village green. Perched on a hilltop about a mile out of town is a great anachronistic ark called the Eagle Mountain House, the kind of place that at first glance seems as if it should have closed when the last steamer trunk was put on the last train, and at second glance looks as if it were opened just yesterday—so thoroughly and impeccably has it been

restored. Curious as to this paradox, I walked into
the lobby on my last visit and found, amidst the Victorian parlor furniture, a floor plan with colored stick
pins inserted by two thirds of the rooms. A talk with
the desk clerk confirmed my suspicions. The Eagle
Mountain House's new owners were selling the units
as condominiums, and to all appearances they were
doing a very brisk business. Here was the secret of all
that restoration financing. And as the old building is
sold piecemeal, it continues to operate as a hotel.
The plan is for condominium owners to notify management two weeks before they intend to occupy
their units, which no one does on anything but a vacation basis. Otherwise, those units are rental rooms
for the transient trade. It's a hotel, it's a condo, it's a
spit-and-polish period piece, complete with health
club and restaurant. So goes entrepreneurship in the
mountains, a century and a half after the first farmers
rented out spare rooms to the first scenery-struck artists and assorted wayfarers.

NORMAN E. EGGERT

Above: *The covered bridge that
leads from Route 16 into
Jackson. At the other end of a
bridge like this, one expects
Brigadoon; Jackson isn't quite
that magical, but it has the
advantage of being there all the
time.*
Left: *A street scene in North
Conway: in the end, Western
civilization came down to
t-shirts.*
Facing page: *The Wentworth
Hotel at Jackson, an elegant old
pile in a lovely village setting.*

GEORGE WUERTHNER

8 Pinkham Notch
Climbing Mt. Washington

When I left Pinkham Notch for the summit of Mt. Washington, it was 60° and raining. It wasn't an especially unpleasant rain—nothing a good poncho wouldn't stand up to—and it had been preceded by a long enough stretch of dry weather so that the Tuckerman Ravine Trail was still firm and unmuddied. All in all, it was a mild October day in the midst of a month of them. But out of respect for my destination, the pack I carried was as heavily loaded, for this day trip up and down the mountain, as it would have been if I had been planning a three-day trek along the Appalachian Trail at lower elevations. I'd brought a woolen turtleneck; extra wool socks, gloves and hat; a compactly-rolled down parka (in addition to the lightweight shell I wore over my sweater); woolen pants; a lightweight one-man tent; a flashlight; a single-burner stove; and a supply of tea, bread, peanut butter and soup. If there was a rescue party in my future, I was determined to be in a position to invite them in for a snack.

Although I'll concede the old-fogie implications of all that goose down and wool (as opposed to the trademarked synthetic body-insulators that have all but replaced them), I don't think I was being a bit overcautious in my general preparations, even on a 60° day dampened by only a little rain. On Mt. Washington, winter can arrive unannounced on an August afternoon. If you climb in October, it's all but certain the weather will change before you are very far from your starting point. At 6,288′, the paterfamilias of the Presidential Range is certainly no titan in a world of Everests, McKinleys and Aconcoguas. But it has more than earned its reputation for having the worst weather in the inhabitated world. For "worst," read "most capricious": spectacular one-time records like the summit's 231-mph wind speed notwithstanding, Mt. Washington's real claim to meteorological notoriety is the swiftness with which its weather can deteriorate. Especially above treeline, there is little telling how quickly conditions can turn from merely inclement to life-threatening, with sud-

den heavy sleet or snow and drastic temperature drops leaving the hiker prey to loss of direction and hypothermia. The rule of thumb on Mt. Washington is that when the weather becomes at all doubtful, turn back; and if a safe retreat is impossible—as in whiteout conditions—make yourself as warm and comfortable as possible and stay where you are. It was to that end that I packed so thoroughly, and with such an apparent sense of overkill.

In addition to sticking out my hand to see that it was raining, I had started the day by checking the morning report of base and summit temperatures and short-term weather predictions at the Appalachian Mountain Club's Pinkham Notch Camp. The "Trading Post," a big room at Pinkham where you can find everything from maps to box lunches to polypropylene underwear (assuming you are not a wool chauvinist) is a traditional starting place for hikers bound for the summit of Mt. Washington and the other peaks of the Presidentials, often by way of one or more of the other seven AMC huts.

Pinkham Notch long has been the favored point of access for trekkers out to explore the heart of the White Mountains. Although no one has reconstructed his precise route with any certainty, it is believed that Darby Field, the first white man to climb Mt. Washington (and very likely the first man of any color, as the Indians lived in awe and fear of the summit as the abode of spirits), followed the Ellis River north at least to the southern reaches of the notch before striking off to the northwest and tacking the peak by way of Boott Spur.

Pinkham is the "oldest" of New Hampshire's three great notches in terms of colonial settlement. There was no road through Franconia Notch before 1805, and while Crawford Notch was discovered in 1771, that was several years after Governors Begging and John Wentworth made major land grants at

---

Facing page: *Peaks of the Presidential Range, seen from the Alpine Garden on Mt. Washington at dawn. The "garden," a natural lawn on the mountain's eastern flank, is at its most beautiful in late June, when Lapland rosebay, alpine azalea and diapensia bloom.*

Conway and North Conway, just south of Pinkham Notch, and only three years before one Captain Evans began hewing a road through Pinkham. (Road-building through Crawford Notch proceeded at a much slower pace, at least in the early years.) The name of the notch, incidentally, is taken from that of Colonel Joseph Pinkham, a settler at Jackson in 1790.

The early settlers of course, largely were content to stick to the valleys and leave the mountains alone. There were exceptions—most notably Ethan Allen Crawford (see Chapter 9), but the white man's first century in the White Mountains was occupied with pursuits such as farming and grazing and the development of north-south trade routes that necessarily skirted the peaks and ridges of the Presidential Range. Pinkham Notch's identity not only as a way station for travelers between Portland and the North Country but as a threshold for hikers and climbers had to await the discovery of the mountains as an attraction in and of themselves. In particular, it had to await the founding of the Appalachian Mountain Club, which eventually would settle upon Pinkham as its northern base of operations.

The Appalachian Mountain Club (AMC) was founded in Boston in 1876. Its organizers were some three dozen members of the academic and scientific communities, interested not merely in "recreation" in the modern sense but in systematic exploration and study of what was still a little-understood mountain region tantalizingly close to Boston. In 1888, just 12 years after the club's founding, the AMC built its first hut for overnight travelers at Madison Springs, in the saddle between Mt. Madison and Mt. Adams.

Madison Springs—expanded in 1911 and 1922 and rebuilt after a fire in 1940—was the first in what was to become by 1965 a chain of eight AMC overnight facilities, not including the hostel established near the site of the old Crawford House in Crawford Notch in the 1980s; the Hermit Lake shelters at Tuckerman Ravine, along the trail between Pinkham Notch and the Mt. Washington summit; and Pinkham Notch Camp itself. Separated by distances of from three to six miles, the huts are generally considered to be a day's leisurely hike from one another, depending on conditions. One benefit they offer is the elimination of tents and major provisions from a hiker's packing list, as each hut, in season, is staffed and equipped to provide dormitory sleeping accommodations and hearty meals. The rustic dining tradition dates to 1906, when a caretaker-cook was installed at Madison Springs.

By 1915, the AMC had huts at Carter Notch, in the divide between Wildcat Mountain and Carter Dome east of Pinkham Notch; and at Lakes of the Clouds, above treeline on the southern shoulder of Mt. Washington. The overall operation, though, still was run out of the club's Boston office. That situation changed in 1920, when the AMC built two cabins on the west side of the road through the notch. Pinkham Notch Camp, as the new compound was called, was to serve both as a bed-and-board link in the hut system and as the club's White Mountains headquarters.

The establishment of Pinkham Notch Camp marked the beginning of the AMC's modern era, in which the full complement of huts would be built, staffed and run as a regular professional operation. But perhaps a better watershed date could be chosen: talk to any old-line "Appie," and chances are you'll be told that the club's place in the mountains was finally defined and made secure with the 1922 hiring of Joseph Brooks Dodge to be hutmaster at Pinkham Notch. Joe Dodge brought to his new job a wonderful knack for getting things done, despite the fact that he had to deal with committees in Boston, on the one hand, and the raw, unchanneled enthusiasm of the young hutmen who came to work for him in the years between the wars. Dodge channeled that enthusiasm splendidly, creating a first-rate staff to run the huts, and he made the most of the resources given him by the AMC hierarchy, taking the initiative whenever, wherever and to whatever extent possible. In 1928 he was put in charge of the huts system as manager, and he almost immediately began laying plans for the westward expansion of the chain of lodges. Lonesome Lake Hut, an existing facility on

state property in Franconia Notch, was incorporated into the system in 1929; in the following year, Dodge helped translate a bequest of funds to the AMC into Greenleaf Hut, on the western flank of Franconia Ridge. Galehead Hut, between Galehead and South Twin mountains in the Pemigewasset Wilderness, was built in 1932, as was the hut at Zealand Falls (see Chapter 9). Meanwhile, the huts at Carter Notch and Lakes of the Clouds were expanded. Somehow, in the midst of supervising all this construction and serving as the gruff but always well loved combination scoutmaster–field marshal–father confessor for the hut crews, Dodge found time to establish the Mount Washington Observatory in 1932.

Joe Dodge ran the AMC's north-country operations until 1959, and continued to make his home in Conway until his death in 1973. He still is spoken of reverentially in AMC circles, more so than any of the august Brahmin founders of the organization. A protean figure and a great lover of life, he was to White Mountains outdoor recreation in the 20th century what Ethan Allen Crawford was to the coming-of-age of innkeeping in the 19th. Each had his niche—and each his notch.

Pinkham Notch Camp today is a bigger, busier affair than the two-cabin establishment Joe Dodge first presided over, bigger even than the expanded cabin with its first "Trading Post" that opened in 1935. The new Trading Post/dining hall building was constructed in 1968, along with the adjacent 120-bed Joe Dodge Lodge and a separate administration building. Here is the logistics center for routine hut and trail crew operations, as well as for the AMC's valued search-and-rescue operations. Hikers who use the huts and and trail system that connects them often take for granted the supply arrangements they depend on. The people who work at Pinkham, though, have a different view of things, and over the years they've seen countless tons of provisions and equipment pass into the notch and onto the trails. A good deal of the packing was done by brute human force; strapping young hutmen (yes, there are hutwomen nowadays too) used to boast of the 100-

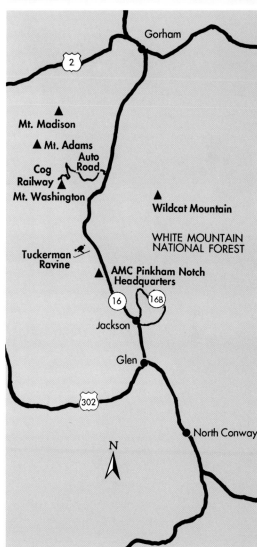

LINDA COLLINS

Facing page: Above treeline on Mt. Washington: the summit, with its weather observatory and television towers, as seen from the Lakes of the Clouds. The Lakes are the site of one of the Appalachian Mountain Club's most popular overnight huts.

pound–plus loads they could shoulder up the trails to the huts. In the 1930s, Joe Dodge brought in mules to do some of the work; they lasted until as recently as 1964. More recently, helicopters have been enlisted for heavy hauling—both of construction supplies and propane on the way up, and waste from self-contained toilets on the way down. With heightened awareness of the vulnerability of the mountain environment, coupled with vastly increased use of the huts, the AMC has begun to practice "clean camping" on an institutional scale. At one hut, solar panels have been installed; at another (Zealand Falls), non-pollution small-scale hydroelectric generation.

Yet for all the expansion of the hut system and improvements in accommodations and provisioning, the actual business of getting around the trail network of the Presidential Range never has gotten less rigorous. To be specific, no one has ever made it one whit easier to walk in the rain from Pinkham Notch Camp to the summit of Mt. Washington by way of Tuckerman Ravine. (As my damp October trek was the first Mt. Washington hike in six or seven years, it occurred to me that some had actually conspired to make it more difficult, although I knew perfectly well that the element responsible was an assemblage of chefs, bakers and confectioners who for all I know have never seen the mountain. These things happen.) The Tuckerman Ravine Trail is by no means among the more demanding of the footpaths through the Presidentials; although it is steep enough on the last stretch above the headwall of the ravine, it can't approach the degree of difficulty offered by a route like the nearby Huntington Ravine Trail, which ascends 650 feet in less than a third of a mile over one stretch, and makes so much use of bare sloping rock that it is best left alone in wet weather. Tuckerman is a bread-and-butter trail, the most popular route from Pinkham to the top of Mt. Washington. Nevertheless, it is a steady grind. On a rainy day when the sun isn't dappling the treetops, it is a reminder of how often the visual component of a hike in the woods is one tenths woods and nine tenths rocks—the ones immediately in front of your feet. The trail below the

Clockwise from upper left:
Heading for the Mt. Washington Summit from Lakes of the Clouds hut.
Autumn in the valley, winter on the mountain: white birches and sugar maples at the foot of Mt. Washington.
The summit of Mt. Washington—and of the north-eastern United States—as certified by the U.S. Geological Survey: 6,288 feet.
Lakes of the Clouds hut. Standing at an elevation above 5,000 feet, the oldest part of the hut dates from 1915.
Facing page: *The Ellis River plunges through a fissure in the rock at Glen Ellis Falls, less than a mile from Route 16 in Pinkham Notch.*

75

ravine is a narrow river of boulders, a glacier's gift to trailbuilders who might otherwise have had to direct the lugged souls of the multitude onto surfaces more fragile and erosion-prone.

When you are hauling yourself uphill at a good pace, you often don't notice a slow but steady drop in temperature. I realized it had gotten colder out when I stopped for tea and a sandwich, at a shelter just downhill from the main buildings at Hermit Lake in the shadow of the Tuckerman headwall. The rain had let up a little, though, and as it was only a little after 11:00 I thought the summit was still a splendid idea. I knew from the weather posting at Pinkham that there was no snow cover up there, and given the capriciousness of the mountain's weather—serenity can arrive as unexpectedly as storms—a bright window of visibility might even open up.

The peanut butter must have gone to my head. In another 10 minutes I was at the little AMC complex at Hermit Lake, with a full view of the vast and symmetrical glacial cirque named for the 19th-century botanist Edward Tuckerman. The caretaker's cabin was boarded shut for the season, but a thermometer hung outside. It read 46°: a 14° drop from the temperature at Pinkham, 2.4 miles and 1,849 feet below. The distance from here to the summit was 1.7 miles, incorporating a gain in elevation of 2,411 feet. Numbers weren't the story, though. As I stood at Hermit Lake the mist that circled the ravine's high, curving headwall parted for a few minutes, leaving only the uppermost rim still hidden. The rain had come back, as hard sleet driven at an angle by the same rising wind that had cleared the mist from the ravine. There were only shades of gray, the colors of autumn turning into winter. The picture had nothing of malevolence about it; that is seldom the opposite of the sunny and benign in nature, even if we allow ourselves the pathetic fallacy. Instead it was sublimely indifferent, and all the more frightening for that. I turned back onto the trail, and headed down to Pinkham Notch.

About a mile and a half below the ravine I saw another hiker for the first time that day. He was in his early 20s, I figured, and he was wearing dungarees, a t-shirt and sneakers. He had a small day pack, and no hat at all. It was raining again, but he had no coat or poncho.

"How far is the summit?" he asked when he got within range. I told him it was about three miles in simple distance, but than in meteorological terms it was getting closer by the minute. By that time, there may well have been snow at Tuckerman.

"I have a sweater in my pack," was all he said.

No doubt he turned around at Hermit Lake. But I wished Joe Dodge had been there, to read him the riot act before the mountain did.

Above: *A hiker looks down into the great glacial cirque known as Tuckerman Ravine.* ***Facing page:*** *A scene along the Tuckerman Ravine Trail, the most popular route to the summit of Mt. Washington.*

NORMAN E. EGGERT PHOTOS BOTH PAGES

9 From Glen to Littleton
By way of Crawford Notch

The grave is at the head of a flight of railway-tie steps laid into the hillside, in a tiny little burial ground set off from the surrounding glade by a fence of stone and iron. The floor of the glade is soft with old evergreen needles; on all sides, there are dense stands of pine. What you see and what you hear in this place are, however, two different things. The pines and the shadowy glade suggest silence, but it is a silence they cannot deliver. Coming from just beyond the trees, on an October day in 1988, were the sounds of hammers and power saws. The graveyard, after all, is barely a third of a mile from Route 302, and between here and the highway you pass a sign that says "Mt. Washington Place Townhomes." The townhomes that day were still a-building, but somehow the noise of construction wasn't entirely inappropriate to the silence of the graveyard in the woods. This is the resting place of Ethan Allen Crawford, the mountain man who, along with his father Abel, invented the tradition of innkeeping in Crawford Notch and blazed the earliest trail to the summit of Mt. Washington. Ethan Crawford might find the valleys a little too crowded for his liking if he were to come back today, and he might be surprised at the number of people who prefer to own their own mountain retreat rather than put up at a hotel. But as he was a Yankee and he was an entrepreneur, he might also be inclined to inquire about a limited partnership in the Mt. Washington Place Townhomes. It was, after all, his pioneering spirit that gave rise to the tourism industry of which the second-home boom is a natural outgrowth.

If you want to travel through the heart of Ethan Allen Crawford's early–19th-century stomping grounds, and the territory in which the grandest of the White Mountains' grand hotels flourished during the century after his death, the road to travel is Route 302 from Glen to Littleton. This is the highway that links the three great north-south notches of New Hampshire; it begins just south of Pinkham, winds through Crawford, and reaches Littleton directly north of Franconia. No other 50-mile stretch of road in New Hampshire simultaneously reveals nearly as much of the state's finest scenery and as many reminders of its most colorful history.

Route 302 branches left from north-south Route 16 at Glen, five miles north of North Conway. Glen scarcely exists as a discernable village; nowadays it's more a motel and service center for the big Attitash ski area, three miles ahead on the left side of the road. Attitash, one of the first New England resorts to install the exhilarating "Alpine Slide" in which summer-season riders pilot a sled-on-wheels down a twisting trough to the base of the mountain, typifies the trend towards year-round utilization of ski trails. Just past the next town of Bartlett, however, the commercial aspect of Route 302 disappears as the highway enters the White Mountain National Forest and veers north toward Crawford Notch.

Although named later in connection with the Crawfords and their celebrated mountain hostelries, Crawford Notch was discovered in 1771 by Timothy Nash, a hunter who had been tracking a moose in the dense forests to the north. Climbing a tree on Cherry Mountain, a peak located in what is now the town of Carroll, Nash looked south to behold the dramatic gap through which the Ammonoosuc and Saco Rivers flow, dividing the heights on either side. Such a north-south route had been widely sought, as a means of access between southern New Hampshire and the new settlements in the far-northern Connecticut Valley, and Nash was quick to report his discovery to Governor John Wentworth. Hesitant to swallow what might be a mountaineer's tall tale, the governor told Nash that his find would entitle him to a land grant north of the notch—if he could get a horse through the difficult passage and on to Portsmouth. With a friend's help, and a very sturdy and obliging horse, Nash met Wentworth's challenge. By 1803, the trail through Crawford Notch was an official state turnpike, predecessor of Route 302.

Facing page: *The Mt. Washington Valley in early autumn, as seen from Intervale. The painter Thomas Cole might have arranged his clouds this way.*

Crawford Notch State Park is a state inholding within the White Mountain National Forest; it begins where Bemis Brook flows into the Saco River, just south of a trail (beginning on the left side of the highway) that leads uphill for one and a half miles to the brook's lovely and secluded Arethusa Falls. Just one mile within the state park, the steep walls of Frankenstein Cliff and the precarious-looking trestle of the Maine Central Railroad are visible, also to the left of 302. The cliff was named for George Frankenstein, an Ohio artist who was a frequent painter of White Mountain scenes.

The road next approaches the site of the best-remembered of all events in the long history of Crawford Notch settlements—the sudden death of nine members of the Willey household, commemorated by a plaque on the site of the Willey House within the state park.

It rained violently up in Crawford Notch on Monday, the 28th of August, 1826. The summer had been hot and dry; the soil on the steep slopes above the valley of the Saco was powdery and precariously loose around the roots of the trees that held the mountainside together. When the heavy rains finally came, they brought the peril of avalanche.

Samuel Willey must have been aware of the danger of slides; according to some versions of the story, he had built a rock shelter downhill from the farmhouse where he lived with his wife and five children. As the tremendous thunderstorm crested on that Monday night, the Willey family heard the sound of an avalanche gathering force on the mountain above them, and they bolted from their house for such shelter as Willey had constructed or hoped to find. None of them—father, mother, children and two hired hands—ever made it to safety.

The avalanche struck a rock ledge 50 yards behind the house, separated and continued on either side of the frame building, burying the Willey family and everything else in its path. The house was left untouched. The next day, when the floodwaters in the valley had subsided, a traveler clambered up to the house. It was empty, with a glass of toddy on the sidebar and a Bible lying open on a table. The Willeys' dog was barking outside. The bodies of Samuel Willey, his wife, the hired men and two of the children were found afterwards; the other three children still lie buried beneath the slide, in the shadow of the mountain since named Mt. Willey.

The Willeys gave their name as well to the brook that flows into the Saco through a 100'-deep ravine in the shadow of Mt. Field. The railway bridge across this ravine, as well as the 500' trestle beneath Frankenstein Cliff (not to be confused with the Frankenstein Trestle on the Mt. Washington Cog Railway), were the work of engineer John Anderson. Together with his brother Samuel, Anderson founded the Portland and Ogdensburg Railroad Company in 1867, with a goal many people said was impossible. They intended to lay track throughout the length of Crawford Notch, thus fully vindicating Governor John Wentworth's dream of a north-south route through the central White Mountains barely a century after its discovery. Getting the iron horse through the notch was a much more formidable task than that which had faced Timothy Nash and his flesh-and-blood horse; in addition to building the bridges and trestles to span a gap such as Willey Brook, the Andersons had to cope with grades that challenged the capabilities of simple-adhesion steam locomotion ("simple adhesion" refers to the pulling power of smooth wheels on smooth tracks, as opposed to the rack-and-gear method of traction used on the Mt. Washington Cog Railway). Over the nine miles leading up to the station at the Crawford House, the elevation gain was a discouraging 1,044', or 116' to the mile. But the Portland and Ogdensburg got through in 1875, and eventually became part of the Maine Central system. Freight trains still operate on the line, although passenger service long since has been abandoned.

That little Crawford House station, a trim Victorian structure on the left side of Route 302 that today serves as an information center for the Appalachian Mountain Club, is a poignant reminder that by the time the railroad came to Crawford Notch, the

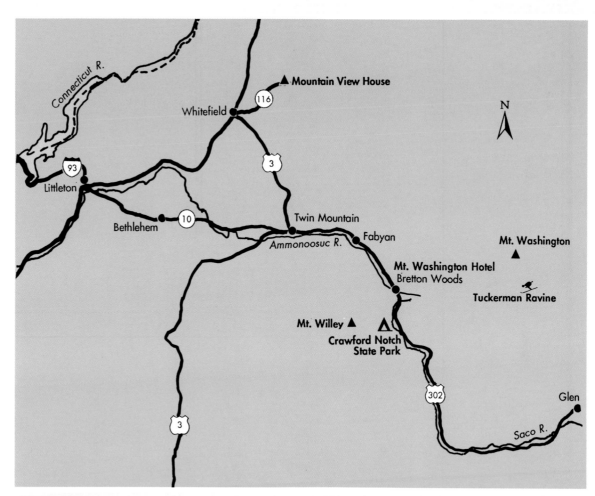

LINDA COLLINS

The hotel-pioneer Crawford family left their name on many features in this area.

Facing page: *Bemis Brook Falls, Crawford Notch State Park. The falls are accessible via the Arethusa Falls Trail from Route 302.*

region was no longer just a place to pass through but a destination in itself. Crawford House, the fabled hotel that stood here in various incarnations until fire ended the succession in 1977, was only one of the great White Mountain resorts—but by direct lineage, it harked back to the origins of north-country innkeeping. The first crude hostelries for wayfarers on the road through Crawford Notch were built by Captain Eleazer Rosebrook and his son-in-law, Abel Crawford, shortly after 1800. In operating his Mount Crawford House, Abel Crawford had the estimable assistance of his strapping son, Ethan Allen. Together the Crawfords not only offered lodging to travelers, but also took time out from their other chores to guide guests to the surrounding summits. In 1819, they built the Crawford Trail to the top of Mt. Washington, and during the early 1820s, Ethan Allen Crawford built the first summit huts on the Presidential Range's loftiest peak.

Crawfords were everywhere, in the early days of what no one had thought yet to call the "hospitality industry," in their namesake notch. The original Mount Crawford House survived until 1876. Another hotel, the Mount Washington House, was the result of the expansion of an 1825 inn built by Ethan Allen Crawford; on its site, in 1873, rose the Fabyan House—destroyed by fire in 1951, and remembered today in the name of a restaurant that occupies its former train station. South of the AMC's (Appalachian Mountain Club) Crawford House Station information center once stood the Notch House, built in 1828 by Abel and Ethan Allen Crawford and managed until it burned in 1853 by Thomas J. Crawford, another son of the pioneer. As for the last and greatest property to bear the Crawford name, it was planned and begun by Tom Crawford, completed in 1852 under now ownership, and rebuilt after an 1859 fire. That was the last Crawford House, the one that burned in 1977.

Although the hotels are gone now, the Crawford name also is perpetuated in the Crawford Path, which is the direct descendant of the 1819 route blazed by Abel and Ethan Allen Crawford. Ac-

NONA BAUER

cording to the Appalachian Mountain Club's *White Mountain Guide*, the 2.9-mile section between the highway and Mt. Pierce is considered to be "the oldest continuously maintained footpath in America." The trail begins on the right side of Route 302 near the Crawford House depot (there is also an AMC-managed hostel, open year-round, a short walk from the depot), and ends 8.2 miles to the northeast at the summit of Mt. Washington. Just 1.7 miles east of Route 302, however, there is a cut-off trail leading right from Crawford Path for 0.7 mile to the AMC's Mizpah Spring Hut, a 60-person facility on the southern flank of Mt. Pierce. (Note: some maps will refer to Mt. Pierce as Mt. Clinton; they are one and the same.) Mizpah Spring Hut is open to the public by reservation from early June through early October, and like all AMC huts offers hearty meals and bunk sleeping accommodations.

Having passed the Crawford House depot, Route 302 descends toward the northern end of Crawford Notch. The passage here is less dramatic than the entry into the notch from the south; ahead the hills are gentler, less abrupt, while to the east the land rises in the successive summits of Mts. Pierce, Eisenhower, Franklin and Monroe, to reach the greatest height in all New England atop the vast, cirque-indented massif of Mt. Washington itself. It is this broad, uncluttered view from the west of the Presidential Range's heart that is the main natural attraction of the place called Bretton Woods.

Bretton Woods was named in 1772 by Governor John Wentworth, after his family's ancient English seat, Bretton Hall. Originally part of a joint land grant made by Wentworth to a group of Portsmouth entrepreneurs (part of this huge parcel was the grant made to Crawford Notch discoverers Timothy Nash and his partner Benjamin Sawyer, who promptly sold their 2,200 acres for roughly $200), Bretton Woods ceased to have any official status when the villages at the northern end of the notch were consolidated as the town of Carroll in 1832. In 1903, though, the post office and railroad station serving the new Mount Washington Hotel were given the old English

Above: *Fresh from a night's stay at the Appalachian Mountain Club's Mizpah Spring Hut, hikers prepare to begin their day's trekking along the Webster Cliff and Mount Clinton trails. The AMC's newest hut (1965), Mizpah has room for 60 overnight guests.*
Left: *Gray fox, near Crawford Notch. Unlike its cousin the wolf, the fox never was extirpated in northern New Hampshire.*
Facing page: *A burst of autumn color north of Crawford Notch.*

TED LEVIN

name. "Bretton Woods" soon came to mean the ulti-mate in luxurious White Mountain lodging, and it eventually would become an instantly recognized name in international diplomatic and economic circles as well.

The Mount Washington Hotel was the last of the great summer resorts of northern New Hampshire to be built, and is the last to remain in operation. It was the creation of railroad speculator Joseph Stick-ney, who bought the old Mount Pleasant House in Crawford Notch and a 10,000-acre tract in the west-ern foothills of Mt. Washington. Here, in 1902, he opened his spare-no-expense Mount Washington Hotel. Built by Italian artisans and laborers who boarded on site throughout the two years of construc-tion, the palatial new resort incorporated steel frame-work, the latest in plumbing, heating and electricity, and its own telephone exchange. Joseph Stickney oversaw the triumphant grand opening (as did Ethan Allen Crawford III) and the first two seasons of op-eration, then died in December of 1903. The little granite Episcopal chapel, which appears on the right side of Route 302 just before the vast white bulk of the hotel itself comes into view in the middle dis-tance, was dedicated to his memory several years af-terward.

Stickney's widow, later the Princess de Lu-cinge, inherited the Mount Washington Hotel and ran it for the next 30 years; since then, a succession of owners managed the property through good times and bad. But in all the nine decades of the hotel's operation, no season has been like the year 1944.

Nineteen forty-four saw the Mount Washing-ton finally pass from Stickney family ownership. Early in that year, the Princess's nephew sold the ho-tel to a group of Boston investors. But before the new management could welcome its first guests of the sea-son, it learned that there would be no guests that year—at least not in the normal sense of the word. The entire hotel was reserved by the United States government, as the site for a conference to shape the economic framework of the postwar world. With vic-tory over the Axis perceived as being only a matter

D. GRUENAU

Above: *Alpine bunch berries provide a touch of ground-level color during summer in the White Mountains foothills.* **Facing page:** *The Mount Washington Hotel, Bretton Woods, grande dame of White Mountains hostelries, now has new owners with a commitment to extensive renovation.*

of time, President Roosevelt and the Allies called representatives of 44 nations to the World Monetary Fund Conference. Their deliberations, held throughout the summer at the Mount Washington Hotel, resulted in the fixing of the gold standard, the adoption of the U.S. dollar as the benchmark against which other national currencies were valued, and the establishment of the World Bank. "Bretton Woods" became the shorthand term by which the conference was known, both in newspaper accounts of the day and in the history of modern economics. The memory of the conference lingers at the Mount Washington today, not only in the form of a memorial plaque but also in the names of individual delegates, posted in brass on the doors of the rooms where they stayed. The practice, incidentally, has continued; prominent individuals from the worlds of politics, sports, the arts and popular entertainment since have been similarly honored. You might take a room at the Mount Washington and find it was the summer-1944 home of the delegate from Mexico, or it may have been the more recent lodgings of a singer or a basketball star.

Like the last of the great transatlantic liners, the Mount Washington Hotel is both a window on a vanished age of luxury and a living reminder that even at this late date, the travel experience has not entirely been flattened to the level of package tours and chain accommodations. The setting alone could not carry Mount Washington if its service and style were not up to snuff; nor could its status as a National Historic Landmark. Fortunately, the syndicates that have run the hotel in recent years have paid attention to detail, and kept a large enough staff (about 350) to do things right.

As of this writing, there has been another recent changing of the guard at Bretton Woods. New owners took charge in 1988, and immediately set an ambitious agenda of renovation. Much of the work being done centers upon plans to make the hotel a year-round resort for the first time, with winter guests to be welcomed beginning early in the 1990s. With heating costs running to $2,000 per day during the month or so prior to the vast building's traditional Columbus Day closing, it's easy to see why insulation, energy-efficient windows and a new heating plant on the premises (the old boiler is located in a separate building, 400 yards away) are top priorities. But so are guest-room refurbishing—including a sad goodbye to the old enameled clawfoot tubs—and a sprucing up of public areas. A long-unused golf course will be re-opened, complementing the beautiful 18-hole links currently in use, and an ice-skating rink will be added to the hotel grounds.

Nearly as many workers are busy with the renovations as were employed to build the hotel in 1902, and like their predecessors they are living at Bretton Woods while the job proceeds. When they are finished, the grand tradition of White Mountains innkeeping should have a new lease on life.

And so we come round to Ethan Allen Crawford once again. The turnoff for his grave is on the right, just past the long drive leading to the Mount Washington Hotel, and past the access road for the Mt. Washington Cog Railway. You'll know you've just passed it if, just after you cross the bridge that spans the Ammonoosuc, you reach the restored railroad depot/restaurant called Fabyan's Station. The graveyard itself is 0.3 mile down the side road—you'll see the railroad-tie steps on the left.

It's fitting that Ethan Allen Crawford should be buried here, a short distance from the site of one of the inns Horace Fabyan bought from him in 1837. Even though financial reverses drove him to a sort of exile in Vermont towards the latter part of his life, his roots were in Crawford Notch and he was most at home among the Presidential peaks he claimed to have named. Along with Allen are interred his pioneer grandfather, Captain Eleazer Rosebrook (1747-1817) and his wife; and Allen's own accomplished wife Lucy (1793-1869), author of the 1846 *History of the White Mountains* that is our source for much of the north country's early history and lore. A simple granite obelisk with the name "Crawford" rises at the center of the plot; nearby is the stone bearing the younger man's inscription:

Above: *The Mt. Washington Cog Railway: an improbable piece of Victorian technology, its trains clank, wheeze and smell like somebody put the Industrial Revolution in a bottle and uncorked it in your face. But it works exactly the way it was planned to, and the views are incomparable.*
Left: *The Cog Railway's ancient locomotives push rather than pull, and make contact not only with the rails but also with a central rack by means of a toothed, ratcheted cog. Each of them could have served as the model for "The Little Engine That Could."*
Facing page: *In Crawford Notch.*

NONA BAUER

*Above: Alpine azalea is an early-summer wildflower of the White Mountains area. **Facing page:** The Ammonoosuc River near Bretton Woods, just north of Crawford Notch. More of a mountain stream in these parts, the Ammonoosuc reaches the Connecticut at Woodsville looking every bit the full-fledged river.*

Ethan Allen Crawford
Died June 22, 1846 Age 52
He built here the first hotel at the White Mountains, of which he was for many years the owner and landlord. He was of great native talent and sagacity, of noble, kind, and benevolent disposition, a beloved husband and father, and an honest and good man.

His grandfather and his father might have argued the point about the first hotel, if indeed the little inns they ran qualified for the term; as for the rest, posterity should treat us all so kindly.

Slightly more than two miles past the Fabyan Depot, a secondary road (open to vehicles from mid-May to mid-November) leads from the left side of Route 302 at Zealand Campground and follows the Zealand River south for three and a half miles. From here, the Zealand Trail continues south for 2.7 miles to Zealand Falls Hut, also an AMC facility, located on a pond at the head of Zealand Notch. Built in 1932, Zealand Falls Hut accommodates 36 hikers, and during summer and early fall provides lodging and meals by reservation. Unlike most of the AMC's White Mountains huts, Zealand Falls is open in the winter; a caretaker takes the place of the full staff, and food must be brought by guests. The hut is popular among back-country cross-country skiers and snowshoers, who make the trek from Route 302 along the relatively level Forest Road and Zealand Trail. The sense of remoteness at Zealand is profound; to the south stretches the vast Pemigewasset Wilderness, with no road of any kind to be reached before the Kancamagus Highway, some 11 miles distant. And the Kancamagus is not open in the winter.

Continue on Route 302 past Fabyan and you are out of Crawford Notch proper. Here the road, like the Maine Central tracks and the Ammonoosuc River, turns to the west. At Twin Mountain, a scant five miles west of Fabyan, you have a choice: continue on directly toward Littleton and the Connecticut Valley, or bear right to follow Route 3 north to Whitefield, from which you can take Route 116 down to Littleton.

The latter option is an interesting one. Route 3 between Twin Mountain and Whitefield offers some of the best mountain scenery north of the notches; although the country up here spreads out, it by no means grows flatter and, if anything, the perspectives are grander because of the sheer distances involved. Just short of 7 miles out of Twin Mountain, the highway crests and reveals a 360° view of the White Mountains to the east and south, the peaks of Vermont's Northeast Kingdom to the west and the isolated ranges of New Hampshire's Coös County to the north.

Whitefield itself is that New England anomaly, a little workaday town, prosperous enough if not opulent at first appearance, that seems to have been little gentrified over the past few decades. Its village center, with a tall bandstand rising from the green, is straight out of Currier and Ives. Whitefield dates to the 1770s, and in the 19th and early 20th centuries went for an economic rollercoaster ride typical of many north-country communities. Products as diverse as potato starch, timber, textiles and condensed milk helped the town prosper, all with the help of excellent rail connections to major New England markets. After the turn of the century, though, Whitefield's economy went into serious decline—a decline stemmed only gradually by the growth of tourism and the town's appeal as a satellite community within reach of Littleton and Berlin.

Just outside Whitefield stands a unique—and, as of this writing, decidedly melancholy—monument to the great age of White Mountains resorts. The Mountain View House, which looms along a narrow road off Route 116 north of town, is the only one of the mountains' great wooden arks to survive fire and the wrecker's ball and yet remain empty and idle. It last welcomed guests in summer 1985, and, although the golf course still is in use and a prospective new owner is trying to get finances and permits in order to reopen the hotel, the rambling, steep-towered structure looks out over its wonderful southerly views without any guests on its verandas or at its windows. The Mountain View House began when a modest

guest wing was built onto a farmhouse in 1865, and by 1906 it had been transformed by a dozen additions into the huge building that stands today. It would be wonderful to see the lights go on in the Mountain View House again—to see, just this once, a reversal of the trend that left the Mount Washington a lone survivor of the days before motels.

If you follow Route 302 directly from Twin Mountain to Littleton, your route will take you through the resort town of Bethlehem, once known as "Bethlehem Street" after its two-mile-long wooden sidewalk lined with more than two dozen hotels. Bethlehem first achieved popularity among summer sojourners during the latter half of the 19th century and rose to prominence largely through the testimonials of hay fever sufferers who found relief here. At one time, the town was even the home of the American Hay Fever Relief Association. A number of locales across New York State and the northern tier of New England have built their reputations on the deliverance they offer to summer-allergy victims. A high concentration of coniferous trees, it seems, creates a natural filtering effect that keeps the pollen count down. In Bethlehem's case, it didn't hurt also to have a fine, open view of the Presidential Range from the west. But whatever its attraction, Bethlehem still is very much in business as a summer resort, even if the sheer number of hostelries along the "street" has diminished since its heyday. The one thing you would not want to be allergic to here, come the warmer months, is golf. It amounts to something of a state religion.

And so into Littleton, the once and future boomtown that stands at the juncture of the upper Connecticut Valley and the roads to the great mountain passes and points north. With its manufacturing economy primed almost from the time of its founding by the abundant water power of the swift-flowing Ammonoosuc River, Littleton thrived as an industrial center throughout the 1800s. One local factory, more than a century ago, turned out 20,000 axes and scythes in a year; another produced nearly a half million pairs of buckskin gloves and mittens a year as recently as the 1940s. Sheep farms in the surrounding rural communities fed Littleton's woolen mills, which worked overtime to weave cloth for uniforms during the Civil War. Distillers and carriagemakers kept busy, and a man named Ben Kilburn with a talent for photographing mountain scenery founded a company that became the largest producer of stereopticon images in the world by the turn of the century.

Littleton's economy has a different base today, but is no less vibrant. Its position as a north-country crossroads and its proximity to Interstate 93—a main thoroughfare for skiers as well as summer vacationers—keep its Main Street lively all year 'round. My last two visits to Littleton were only one year apart, but that short period saw the opening of a major new restaurant/bar/retail complex downtown, complete with the requisite postmodernist architectural touches.

As a respite from this up-to-the-minute syndrome, I always prefer to spend my nights in Littleton at a place that has seen it all, from homemade hard cider to the latest designer beers. Thayer's Inn, on Main Street, is a stately Greek-Revival hostelry that has been in business since 1843. It isn't the Mount Washington Hotel, nor does it try to be; it belongs instead to that vanishing breed of small-town hotels that have steadfastly resisted the pressure to become either fleabags or parking lots. The public rooms are impeccably Victorian, the accommodations simple but tidy and wonderfully inexpensive. Best of all, you can go up into the cupola, five stories above the street, and look out at the town and the hills that surround it. Dawn is a fine time to climb the stairs to the top of Thayer's, and so is dusk; when Littleton is quiet, you can hear the rush of the Ammonoosuc behind the buildings along Main Street. It is almost to the Connecticut now, and has come a long way from its source, high up in Crawford Notch.

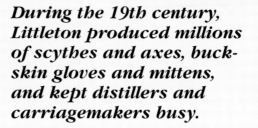

During the 19th century, Littleton produced millions of scythes and axes, buckskin gloves and mittens, and kept distillers and carriagemakers busy.

Above: Thayer's Inn in downtown Littleton preserves one room just as it looked when the hostelry opened, but retains its Victorian air throughout.
Left: Thayer's Inn celebrates its sesquicentennial in 1993. This was a favored resort of actors and actresses back when the railroad brought traveling theatrical productions to the Littleton Opera House.
Facing page: Littleton, a 19th-century manufacturing center born again as a mecca for skiers and summer visitors. Interstate 93 helped put it back on the map.

10 From Colebrook to the Connecticut Lakes

Look for it on the right side of Route 3, on the grounds of the Shrine of Our Lady of Grace as you approach the southern outskirts of Colebrook. In a state that prides itself on its granite, this may be the most unusual statue ever chiseled from stone. Called "Motorcyclists in Prayer," it is a lifesize depiction of a man and a woman kneeling in devout contemplation beside their bike, a big highway cruising model that looks oddly immobile in this medium. Their granite duffels are strapped over the rear wheel, and a granite Bible lies open before them. On the plinth beneath them are the dedication and the name of the sculptor, John M. Weidman, Jr., along with a list of the individuals, clubs and companies who paid for the massive carving.

There is nothing out of the ordinary about the rest of the shrine, with its well kept lawns, fountain, votive-lighted altar and benches for Mass, and statues of the Blessed Virgin. It is run by the Oblate Fathers, or Le Peres Oblate as the sign says in a reminder of the nearness of French Canada, and across the road are a chapel, a religious articles shop, and a trail marked by the Stations of the Cross. On the October day when I was last in Colebrook, there were no motorcycles at the shrine.

Why are this granite pair and their machine planted on the threshold of Colebrook, the largest town in the far northern tip of New Hampshire? Because every year, in late spring, hundreds of motorcyclists from throughout New England ride to Colebrook for the blessing of the bikes. The origins of this ritual are lost in the mists, but it always takes place at the Shrine of Our Lady of Grace, and that's where cycling enthusiasts of religious turn of mind decided to place the statue. In these parts it could have been a granite deer hunter, or a granite snowmobile, or in times gone by a granite lumberjack. But the motorcyclists were better organized, and they got here first.

Colebrook may be the bikers' destination, a sort of ultima Thule at the end of all the roads leading from the populated underbelly of New England, but it makes a wonderful starting-off point as well.

Although it is only an hour's drive from Colebrook through the farthest nub of Coös County to the Canadian border, the trip can easily be stretched to a day's exploration or more. It takes in some of New Hampshire's least-visited wilderness and one of its most luxurious hotels; it traverses what was once a bitterly contested no-man's-land only to end at one of the world's most peaceful frontiers. It is also a journey to a source, to the trickling headwaters of the stream the Abnaki called Quinn-attuck-auke, "The Long Deer Place," and which we call the Connecticut River. And the trip begins, oddly enough, with a look at the only stone motorcycle in New England. We hesitate to say the United States, because that includes California.

Colebrook, situated at the confluence of the tiny Mohawk River with the Connecticut, grew up as a lumbering center and market town for outlying farms. Although its population is barely above 1,000, it has the busy main street of a town 10 times its size, if only because the hinterlands of northern Coös have nowhere else to trade: if you live up here and you want to buy a lawn mower or an engagement ring or an aerobics video, you come to Colebrook, where the retail environment is fixed in time about a decade before the building of the first shopping mall. But America's vanishing Main Streets, when you think of it, were our first shopping malls.

Beyond the old hotel on the north end of town the houses and stores thin out quickly, and Route 3 meanders on with the infant Connecticut on its left. The river can't be more than 50 feet across here, and the Vermont cows on the other side seem as if they could casually wade across and change their citizenship. Vermont's Mt. Monadnock, a 3,140′ namesake of the slightly taller peak in southern New Hampshire, is the dominant feature of the surrounding landscape; on this side of the river, the hills are lower and farther apart, faint suggestions of the summits

Facing page: Main Street, Colebrook. Note the big elm tree on the left, a survivor of Dutch Elm Disease that devastated the lordly canopies that once covered New England streets like this one.

GEORGE WUERTHNER

that guard the great notches to the south. Once you lift your eyes above the dairy farms in the foreground, the sense you get north of Colebrook is of being in the mountains rather than in the woods.

Just past Stewartstown—a scant collection of houses with a bridge across the Connecticut to Canaan, Vermont—a roadside marker identifies 45° North Latitude, the line halfway between the Equator and the North Pole. For seven or eight months of the year in these parts, the concept of equidistance between these two entities seems like a bad joke; anyone would bet that it would be a much shorter drive from here to the Pole than to Ecuador. But this is Forty-five, a demarcation of some political importance even if its climatic implications are largely symbolic. It was the latitude chosen in the 1842 Webster-Ashburton Treaty as the boundary between Canada and the United States, to a point as far east as Hall's Stream, a south-flowing tributary of the Connecticut. From there (a spot in the forest just west of Route 3, where Quebec, Vermont and New Hampshire meet), the frontier follows Hall's Stream north, allowing New Hampshire to reach a higher latitude than straight-bordered Vermont. This arrangement wrote finis to a thorny little chapter in the history of the North Country, as we'll see when we get to Pittsburg.

If you look west across the river at the Stewartstown latitude marker, though, that's not Canada but Beecher Falls, Vermont that you see. Border surveying must have been a less exact science back when the line was drawn, since Canada actually starts about a mile north of here.

But Route 3 stays with the Connecticut proper from here on, with New Hampshire on both sides. The largest town in New Hampshire, in fact: this is Pittsburg, unsurpassed in acreage (and close to dead last in population) among all the Granite State's municipalities. There's hardly anything at all to the town; a couple of general stores, a school, a gas station, a handful of houses and a year-round, log-cabin information center which, the last time I visited, was staffed by a sprightly 80-year-old woman who not

GERARD LEMMO

only allowed as to how she'd been out bird hunting the day before, but even gave me her recipe for partridge pie (you use biscuit dough for the crust). But if all this seems just the bare bones of a rural community, think of how it would measure up as an independent nation! That's just what Pittsburg was, for a time in the early 1830s: the Republic of Indian Stream.

New Hampshire chronicler Ella Shannon Bowles once called the political framework of Indian Stream "the most democratic form of independent government ever known in the Western World," and more than likely it was. How could it be otherwise, with a population of some 360 souls, and every voter among them a member of the legislature? What prompted the creation of this remote and miniature republic was the inability of American and British diplomats to agree on the question of which stream was the northwesternmost of the sources of the Connecticut. Ever since England recognized the independence of her former colonies, it had been accepted that that waterway would form the boundary between New Hampshire and Canada. Trouble was, which stream was it? The Americans lobbied for Indian Stream, which is actually the next-to-northwesternmost; and the British built their case around the fledgling river that links what we now call the Connecticut Lakes. Each side took its interpretation of the boundary seriously enough to attempt to extend political control over the disputed area, and over the lives of the farmers and assorted backwoodsmen who made their homes there. This meant that while the magistrate at Hereford, Quebec was attempting to draft the settlers into the militia, the sheriff of Coös County was trying to tax the produce they exported. The situation came to a head in the summer of 1832, when the Republic of Indian Stream declared its independence.

This brave political act cut no ice with the United States or Great Britain, which exercised power on behalf of its colony Canada. Authorities on both sides of the disputed border continued to consider it their prerogative to serve writs within the republic; at one point, Canadian officials even at-

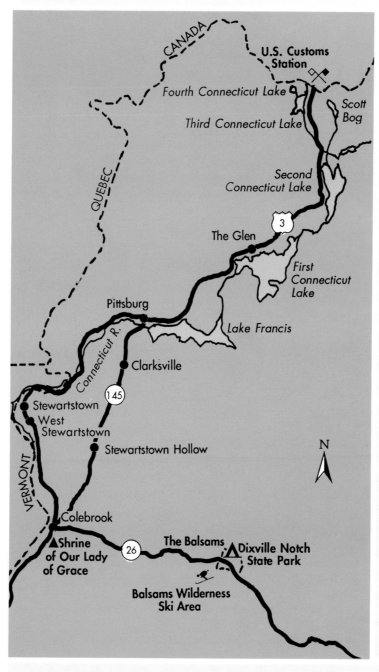

In the summer of 1832, the Republic of Indian Stream—having had enough of the boundary dispute—declared its independence from both the United States and Canada.

Facing page, top: Pittsburg was the capital of the Republic of Indian Stream, a "mouse that roared" against both Canada and the United States. Actually, Pittsburg was the republic.
Bottom: "Motorcyclists in Prayer," Colebrook. The statue stands on the grounds of Our Lady of Grace Shrine, along Route 3.

95

tempted to arrest Luther Park, president of Indian Stream. The "Indian Stream War" started and ended without fatalities when a Coös County sheriff's deputy was seized by Canadian sympathizers and nearly carted off across the border before being rescued by the New Hampshire faction.

Factionalism, as it turned out, had sapped Indian Stream's viability as much as any outside pressure. There was a party favoring union with Canada, and another willing to cast its lot with New Hampshire. The small party of "nationalists" was lost somewhere in the middle. In 1835, the year of the "war," the state sent its militia to restore order. After another five years of nominal independence, during which most of the Canadian faction voted with their feet by moving to Quebec proper, the Indian Stream legislature in its last official act opted to join New Hampshire. The matter came to a formal close with the adoption of the Webster-Ashburton Treaty in 1842.

At any point between Pittsburg and the Canadian border you are likely to pass a heavily-laden logging truck, a reminder that farming long since has been eclipsed by timber harvesting in far-northern New Hampshire. The forest holdings amassed by the great paper companies over the past century comprise a swath of Vermont, New Hampshire and Maine so vast as to constitute a nation-within-a-nation that would dwarf the Republic of Indian Stream, and which in its way is far more autonomous. Ownership and maintenance of this territory purely for its logging potential have paradoxically assured the survival of much of it as wilderness; only a fraction of a paper firm's property is being cut any any given time, and corporate policy has generally been favorable to campers, hikers, hunters and fishermen.

Over the past few years, though, a new trend in North Country land use has emerged. The big outfits that own so much of the tri-state area's northern tier are deciding to divest themselves of much of their acreage, now that land values even in these remote regions are being driven upward by development pressures. In February 1988, Diamond International Corporation put nearly 1 million acres on the market, and between 10 and 30 million acres reaching all the way to New York State are expected to come up for sale by the end of the century. Although nearly a tenth of Diamond International's 1988 offering was in New Hampshire, a Nashua developer came close to purchasing all of it. Fortunately, a funding package put together by the state of New Hampshire with the assistance from the federal government enabled to state to buy 45,500 acres of the property for preservation, as open land and wildlife habitat. But whether conservationists come out ahead in the many rounds to follow depends on the success of a federal study, involving representatives of four states, the timber industry, and organizations such as the Nature Conservancy, aimed at setting policy governing what appears to be nothing less than the eventual disposition of the North Woods.

Whoever ends up owning the forests of northern New England, their ultimate survival may be in other hands…or in all our hands. When I last drove through upper Coös County, it was a late October day, and I thought I had left autumn's lingering displays of foliage far to the south. But suddenly, on rounding a bend outside of Colebrook, I saw a great spray of yellow that I took to be a stand of birches in all their glory. Driving closer, though, I saw that they weren't birches. They were spruce—they were evergreen trees. If we need further study to determine the effects of acid rain, perhaps we need a study to learn if fire burns.

Continue past Pittsburg, and you come upon proof that the rise and fall of farming and logging have by no means been the only major influences on the lay of this lonely land. Hydro power is another shaper of geography. To the right of Route 3 north of Pittsburg villages lies Lake Francis, which was created by damming the Connecticut between the points where Perry Stream and Indian Stream join the river proper, itself no more than a stream above and below the man-made lake. Lake Francis State Park at the northern tip of the lake is accessible by a gravel road from Route 3. Partway along the park road stands an old covered bridge across Perry

GERARD LEMMO PHOTOS

Above: Hydro dam, First Connecticut Lake. The lakes obviously were numbered by settlers moving from south to north; logically, the "first" should be the northernmost lake in the chain, which is the true source of the Connecticut River. But that little pool is called the Fourth Connecticut Lake, and no one is going to renumber them.

Left: A young bull moose in velvet—not an uncommon sight in this part of New Hampshire. The "velvet" is actually a covering within which tiny blood vessels carry nutrients to the antlers, as part of their annual growth cycle.

Facing page: Along Lake Francis, Pittsburg. The fledgling Connecticut River emerges from the western end of this man-made lake.

97

GERARD LEMMO PHOTOS BOTH PAGES

Above: *Cabins at The Glen, a quiet retreat on the western shore of the First Connecticut Lake.*
Right: *The dining room at The Glen. The cuisine here is inspired by fresh air and hearty appetites, and not by the latest trends in Los Angeles.*
Facing page: *Almost to Canada: Second Connecticut Lake.*

Stream, right next to the concrete span that replaced it. There are trout in the river below, but they may be taken—as the sign on the covered bridge says—by fly fishing only. I stood just downstream from a clearly visible school of about 40 of them on a June morning, laying out line after line tipped with every nymph and dry fly in my book, to no more effect than if I had been skipping stones. This is the kind of tantalizing that supposedly keeps fishing from being boring.

The park road ends at a pretty grove of trees and picnic tables, with campsites, right on the shore of Lake Francis. This is the first of a string of access points for recreational use of the Connecticut Lakes, the next two being boat launch and picnic sites maintained by the New England Power Company near its dams on First Connecticut Lake (the next large body of water you encounter if you're continuing north on Route 3), and Second Connecticut Lake (a few miles farther along, after the highway enters George O. Roberts State Park). The two numbered lakes were dammed and thus enlarged in 1930 and 1934, respectively, and are stocked with trout and landlocked salmon.

Along the western shore of First Connnecticut Lake is a lodging place that has always impressed me as a throwback to a more genteel era in wilderness accommodations. It's called The Glen, and unlike some of the other local establishments that cater to a hunting as well as a fishing clientele, it is open only from late spring to early autumn. The Glen is a loose cluster of lakeside cabins set among birches and pines, with a big, rambling main lodge where guests' meals are served (the public is welcome at dinnertime by reservation). The lodge features a big fireplace, a library and a stack of board games; down at the dock is a livery with outboards and canoes—from here it is a paddle of only minutes to quiet coves bordered by the silent and unbroken forest. Pitching a tent at the end of a long portage is one way to appreciate the woods, and I'm happy to do it when I have the chance. But I've come to enjoy taking my loon sounds from the porch of a cozy cabin, after pot roast and a round of Scrabble in the lodge.

NONA BAUER

If you were to have driven past The Glen and the southern tip of Second Connecticut Lake before 1939, you would have run out of road. Not even the patched-over, frost-heaved blacktop that passes for a federal highway here today reached beyond the Second Lake until that year, when a crew of Civilian Conservation Corps boys completed the road through to the border. Back in those days, a trip to the Third Connecticut Lake (the farther north, the higher the number) would have meant a good five-mile slog; now, the Third Lake drifts into view on the left side of the road right after you pass the state's Moose Falls campsite. But the ultimate prize for collectors of farthest sources—for anyone who has read Alan Moorehead's *The White Nile* and who owns a pair of hiking boots—still is tucked safely in the sticks, nearly three quarters of a mile from the pavement at an altitude of 2,605 feet. This is a boggy little pond called the Fourth Connecticut Lake, and it is where Quinn-attuck-auke begins its long southward flow to Long Island Sound.

According to the Appalachian Mountain Club's *White Mountain Guide,* the best place from which to set out for Fourth Lake is the U.S. Customs station, located directly on the border on the left side of Route 3. From here it's a six-tenths-of-a-mile hike along the border to marker 484-15, from which point you bushwhack in a south-southwesterly direction for another tenth of a mile to reach the secluded pool, lying 75 feet below the summit of 2,675' Mt. Prospect.

The distance from the road is insignificant, but finding Fourth Lake can be a daunting task nonetheless. For one thing, it's easy to think you're hiking along the border when you're not. A snowmobile trail, blazed at intervals with orange diamonds set on a white background, leaves the highway at almost the same point as the border swath. I once walked this trail for what must have been well beyond 0.6 of a mile, only to look off to my left and see, through the pines, a large expanse of water that was clearly Third Lake. This meant that the Fourth Lake was hidden in the forest somewhere uphill and to my right, between my bare-ground snowmobile route

GEORGE WUERTHNER

and the actual border. Given the lateness of the afternoon hour, I decided to leave it there, undiscovered, until the next time I'm in upper Coös.

The other problem with the prescribed route to Fourth Lake is that even if you pick up the border at Route 3, it isn't the easiest thing to follow. The authorities clear the swath every 10 years or so, and if you happen by when it needs a serious trim you may have a hard time staying on track, let alone finding the little brass and concrete marker numbered 484-15. If Robert Frost was right about good fences making good neighbors, this "fence" is surely the exception. Seldom have two nations been better neighbors, but seldom—except maybe along the Brazil-Venezuela frontier in the Amazon jungle—has an international boundary been kept in more haphazard repair.

If you try to find Fourth Lake, though, do take the border seriously and report your intentions to the customs agents on the U.S. side. They should be able to tell you just where the border swath meets the road, and they'll remind you to wear bright colors if hunting season is on. Also, if you make your presence known you're less likely to be suspected of a furtive border crossing when you're spotted entering or leaving the woods.

Whether you've made it to Fourth Lake or not, the paucity of roads north of Pittsburg means that you will have to return the way you came, on U.S. 3. At Pittsburg, though, you have an option of heading south to Colebrook on what I consider one of the half-dozen best roads in New England, both for scenery and loop-the-loop driving fun: State Route 145.

Route 145 covers only 15 miles between Pittsburg and Colebrook, by way of the hamlets of Clarksville and Stewartstown Hollow, but along the way it dips and turns past a sequence of magnificent vistas—rolling dairyland in the foreground (be careful of farmers taking their cows across the road at milking time), and the remote peaks of Vermont's Northeast Kingdom in the distance. The remarkable thing about the views along 145 is their all-inclusiveness; they take in the salient features of so many

GERARD LEMMO

GEORGE WUERTHNER

Above: *Scott Bog, Pittsburg—one source of the Connecticut River, which flows from northernmost New Hampshire to Long Island Sound. It is New England's longest river, and, as a pathway of settlement, by far its most important.* **Left:** *Near Clarksville, between Pittsburg and Colebrook along Route 145.*
Facing page, top: *Lake Francis.* **Bottom:** *A Connecticut Valley farm near Colebrook, on the New Hampshire side of the river. In the background is Vermont's Mt. Monadnock, not to be confused with the southern New Hampshire mountain of the same name.*

points between the viewer and the horizon that the effect is a tour de force of depth perception. The landscape just spills away, from the dashboard to the horizon, and the level country outside of Colebrook comes up all too soon.

It won't do to end this excursion back in Colebrook without a side trip—10 miles each way, via State Route 26—to Dixville Notch and the Balsams. Dixville in the northernmost of New Hampshire's four great notches, or mountain passes; it slices through the height of land separating the Connecticut Valley from the drainage basin of the wild Androscoggin. The steep, craggy walls of the notch keep the narrow highway in near-perpetual shadow.

The Balsams Grand Resort Hotel stands just west of the notch proper, nearly 1,000 feet below the cliffs that surround man-made Lake Gloriette. Like Dixville Notch, the Balsams too is the farthest north of its kind in New Hampshire, an outpost of old-style mountain hotel luxury in terms of location as well as time. The oldest portion of what is now a 400-guest operation dates to 1873, and by the first decade of this century, most of what was to become a 15,000-acre setting for the hotel had been acquired from a paper company. But most of the great hotels of the White Mountains and the North Country became anachronisms by the postwar era, as did such immense private forest landholdings, and the Balsams ended up on the block in a federal foreclosure auction in 1954. The integrity of the resort and the property were preserved, though, when a Massachusetts rubber products manufacturer named Neil Tillotson purchased the land and buildings and set about proving that at least here in Dixville Notch, the old traditions could survive. (As of this writing, the Mount Washington Hotel in Bretton Woods is the only other survivor of the golden age of lavish mountain innkeeping in New Hampshire.)

Tillotson made his resort into a year-round operation with the opening of the Wilderness ski area in 1966, while the hotel's reputation as a destination for summer travelers largely has been founded on the incomparably scenic setting of its 18-hole Panorama

Golf Course, set amidst rolling hills surrounded by the peaks that gird Dixville Notch. Even people who have never been to either the hotel or the notch are aware of the place at least every four years, when Dixville is the first community to vote in the New Hampshire primary and the presidential election—in fact, the midnight rituals take place in a meeting room right in the hotel's main building. What even a good many Balsams guests don't know, however, is that Neil Tillotson runs his rubber business out a cluster of unobtrusive buildings right behind the hotel. Here several hundred employees turn out 10 of millions of latex medical examination gloves and toy balloons each year; it's clean, quiet work, and doesn't impinge on the resort setting.

If a guest or a traveler passing along Route 26 should want a few balloons, though, the Balsams is the place to find them. I stopped in one day in late October, when the hotel was closed for its post-foliage, pre-Christmas hiatus, and found that the gift shop was open for business through Halloween. Along one wall was a display of glass jars holding more balloons than I had ever seen in one place— jack-o-lantern balloons, long thin balloons for twisting into animal shapes, balloons with numbered birthday and anniversary tidings printed on them, balloons stamped with nearly every first name in circulation, and balloons in un-balloonlike deep colors including gold and silver. But there was one item in particular I was looking for, and didn't see right away. I called to the young sales clerk and asked her if the store stocked Tilly's Cat Balloon. "Right here," she said, showing me a bowl full of round balloons with perky ears and smiling cat faces. I remembered them from childhood, and had recently read that Mr. Tillotson first produced his latex cat in 1931.

"He's been making these a long time, hasn't he," I said to the clerk.

"Yes," she answered. "That was my grandfather's first novelty balloon."

And so the old Yankee ethos lives. There may be thousands of acres out there, but you start out by selling thousands of balloons.

GERARD LEMMO

Above: *The Balsams Hotel, Dixville Notch, in midsummer. Lake Gloriette is in the foreground; the hills beyond the hotel are part of the 15,000 acres that make up this magnificent resort.*
Left: *The Connecticut River on its journey through Coös County.*
Facing page: *Norton Pool, near the Canadian border among the headwaters of the Connecticut.*

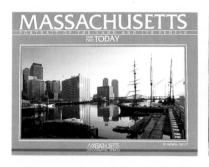

EACH BOOK HAS
ABOUT 100
PAGES, 11"x 8 $\frac{1}{2}$",
120 COLOR
PHOTOGRAPHS

Enjoy, See, Understand America State by State

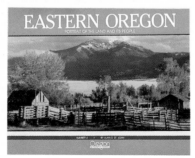

Geographic Series of the States
American Geographic Publishing

Lively, colorful, beautifully illustrated books specially written for these series explain land form, animals and plants, economy, lifestyle and history of each state or feature. Generous color photography brings each state to life and makes each book a treat to turn to frequently. The geographic series format is designed to give you more information than coffee-table photo books, yet so much more color photography than simple guide books.

Each book includes:
* *Colorful maps*
* *Valuable descriptions and charts of features such as volcanoes and glaciers*
* *Up-to-date understanding of environmental problems where man and nature are in conflict*
* *Reference for additional reading, agencies and offices to contact for more information*
* *Special sections portraying people in their homes, at work, in the countryside*

for more information write:
American Geographic Publishing
P.O. Box 5630
Helena, Montana 59604